HOPE,
HUMAN
AND
WILD

HOPE, HUMAN AND WILD

TRUE STORIES OF LIVING
LIGHTLY ON THE EARTH

Bill McKibben

MILKWEED EDITIONS

Published 2007 by Milkweed Editions
Printed in Canada
Cover design by Christian Fuenfhausen
Cover photo by Peter Langer
Interior design based on original hard cover edition; newly composed by Dorie McClelland, Spring Book Design
The text of this book is set in Adobe Jenson.
07 08 09 10 11   5 4 3 2

Milkweed Editions, a nonprofit publisher, gratefully acknowledges sustaining support from Emilie and Henry Buchwald; Bush Foundation; Patrick and Aimee Butler Family Foundation; Cargill Value Investment; Timothy and Tara Clark Family Charitable Fund; Dougherty Family Foundation; Ecolab Foundation; General Mills Foundation; John and Joanne Gordon; Greystone Foundation; Institute for Scholarship in the Liberal Arts, College of Arts and Sciences, University of Notre Dame; Constance B. Kunin; Marshall BankFirst; Marshall Field's Gives; May Department Stores Company Foundation; McKnight Foundation; a grant from the Minnesota State Arts Board, through an appropriation by the Minnesota State Legislature, a grant from the National Endowment for the Arts, and private funders; an award from the National Endowment for the Arts, which believes that a great nation deserves great art; Navarre Corporation; Debbie Reynolds; St. Paul Travelers Foundation; Ellen and Sheldon Sturgis; Target Foundation; Gertrude Sexton Thompson Charitable Trust (George R. A. Johnson, Trustee); James R. Thorpe Foundation; Toro Foundation; Serene and Christopher Warren; W. M. Foundation; and Xcel Energy Foundation.

Library of Congress Cataloging-in-Publication Data

McKibben, Bill.
Hope, human and wild : true stories of living lightly on the earth / Bill McKibben.
    p. cm.
    Originally published: Boston : Little, Brown and Co., c1995.
    ISBN-13: 978-1-57131-300-3 (pbk. : alk. paper)
    ISBN-10: 1-57131-300-1 (pbk. : alk. paper)
  1. Environmental degradation. 2. Nature—Effect of human beings on. 3. Adirondack Mountains (N.Y.)—Environmental conditions. 4. Curitiba (Brazil)—Environmental conditions. 5. Kerala (India)—Environmental conditions. I. Title.
  GE140.M35 2007
  304.2'8—DC22

          2006023504

This book is printed on acid-free, recycled (100% post consumer waste) paper.

For Sophie, of course

A part of our obligation to our own being and to our descendants is to study life and our conditions, searching always for the authentic underpinnings of hope.

—WENDELL BERRY

Contents

Acknowledgments

I am grateful to many people and institutions for their help with this book first to David Brower, who told me the year I published *The End of Nature* that I needed to follow it with a volume about "renewal, recovery, restoration." He was right, and not for the first time.

The generosity of the Guggenheim Foundation made much of the necessary travel possible. When we visited Curitiba, Eliana Maria V. Stabile was our fixer and facilitator; and many of that city's writers, thinkers, and municipal leaders were our hosts, including Cristavao Tezza, Valencio Xavier, Oswaldo Alves, Ester Proveller, and Christine Braga. To Jaime Lerner I am grateful not only for granting me several interviews and access to many other people, but also for his key role in creating a city that was a gracious home for our many weeks there.

In India I was especially grateful for an astute traveling companion, Dr. Martin Fergus. Will Anderson of the Food First Institute put me in touch with Dr. P. K. Nambiar, who made many of the arrangements for my visit—including finding me the perfect place to stay, the Mitraniketan compound run by Mr. Vishwanathan.

The graciousness of his hospitality, and the strength of his experience, will long remain with me. My understanding of Kerala was greatly helped by the time I spent at the Centre for Development Studies in Trivandrum, and especially by the wise counsel of Dr. Richard Franke, an American academic whose works on Kerala were my constant companions, and which I recommend to anyone interested in more information on the topic.

My travels, both physical and intellectual, in the American East were assisted by many friends and neighbors. In the Adirondacks, these include Chris Shaw, John Collins, George Davis, Paul Schaefer, Dr. John Rugge, Ted Caldwell, Michael Wilson, and Duane Ricketson; elsewhere I am indebted to Jamie Sayen not only for sharing his own experiences, but also for publishing the *Northern Forest Forum*, a new periodical of great value. Similar thanks to John Davis, Marcia Cary, Kathleen Fitzgerald, Tom Butler, and the others at *Wild Earth*, and to Brownie Newman, Brent Connor, and their colleagues in the southern Appalachians. Rudy Engholm and the Environmental Air Force provided me with a brand-new vision of many places; Mitch Lansky shared the great volume of research he compiled while writing *Beyond the Beauty Strip*, the most compelling account to date of industrial forestry; Gary Lawless, Samuel and Elizabeth Smith, John Harrigan, Fred King, Sharon Francis, Michael Phillips, Scott Thiele, and many others were also generous with their time and their thoughts. I'm also deeply grateful to Brooke and Terry Tempest Williams, for pointing out the divisiveness of the contrast between East and West in the original manuscript; they are true, tough friends.

As I considered visions of a possible future for the place where I live, I drew on the best things about its present: for me this includes the fellowship of the men and women of the Johnsburg United Methodist Church and its pastors, Barb Lemmel and Mitch Hay, as well as the mountains and woods around our house, so ably patrolled by forest ranger Steve Ovitt.

My editor, Jim Silberman, deserves great thanks for nurturing this book and helping to divine the often-hidden intentions of the first draft. His colleagues Nine Evtuhov, Katey Long, and Beth Davey also have my gratitude, as does Stephen Lamont for his superb copyediting. As usual, my agent, Gloria Loomis, was the real sparkplug behind this project; she is the best help a writer could have. Her able colleagues, Nicole Aragi and Lily Oei, were also of great assistance.

Bill Whitworth, Corby Kummer, Sue Parilla, and many others at the *Atlantic* helped enormously in the task of editing and checking portions of the eastern forests section. Similarly, I am grateful to Bob Coles, Alex Harris, Jay Woodruff, Liz Phillips, and Maura High at *Doubletake* magazine for their work on the Kerala material, and to Reed McManus, Jonathan King, Roger Cohn, Michael Hirschorn, and James Atlas, who edited other magazine pieces inspired by this volume. I would also like to thank the crew at Milkweed Editions for bringing this book back into print.

This book would never have been written if Elaine Good-speed and Jackie Vetter-Avignon hadn't been willing and able to help with Sophie Crane McKibben and it wouldn't have been written, I think, if Sophie hadn't presented me with a deep reason to look and work for a more hopeful future. It is for Sophie and for her mother, my ablest coworker and best friend, Sue Halpern that this book was written.

HOPE,
HUMAN
AND
WILD

Introduction

For those concerned about the environment, this is a strange season of waiting, a hard time for hope. A few months after the Clinton administration took office, I interviewed Vice President Al Gore, and he said something that stuck in my mind: "We are in an unusual predicament as a global civilization. The maximum that is politically feasible, even the maximum that is politically *imaginable* right now, still falls short of the minimum that is scientifically and ecologically necessary." And that was in the optimistic early days of Clinton's presidency. I finished this manuscript in January of 1995, as Newt Gingrich and the Republicans took formal control of Congress, intent on watering down the environmental laws we already have.

So you could say my timing is off. In this book I try to imagine a future vastly different from the present, one where people consume much less and restrain themselves much more. Where "public" is no longer a curse word, and "growth" increasingly is. Despite the examples that fill these pages, the chances of such a world seem small just now: we are heading in the opposite direction, and fast.

And yet there is another sense in which my timing may be right. Like a comet orbiting the earth, widespread concern for the environment swings into view only periodically. The time of Rachel Carson, culminating in the first Earth Day, for instance, or the furor over the greenhouse effect that peaked on Earth Day's twentieth anniversary. In between, when political action is unlikely, come quieter moments for laying plans, for collecting the ideas and solutions that will form the basis of the next environmental debate.

For that debate will surely come again, that comet will swing back into view. For better and for worse, all the inspired rhetoric of the resurgent Right cannot change the physical facts of the planet's deterioration; Rush Limbaugh's bluster, sadly, is no match for the gathering pall of greenhouse gases. Attack ads and spin doctors can't change the molecular structure of carbon dioxide. On the twenty-fifth day of the new Congress, when the House passed the balanced budget amendment to the Constitution, a small story in the paper noted an announcement from the world's climate researchers that global temperature had resumed the steady upward climb briefly halted by the eruption of Mount Pinatubo. Within a few short years, the world will have much larger problems to face than budget deficits.

And when that renewed concern inevitably emerges, we will need ideas on the table more far-reaching than recycling. From the environmental crisis must emerge a new politics, one that goes beyond the pipe dreams of Left and Right and especially Center. This book, the story of a journey, is filled with such ideas, each of them difficult but each of them drawn from real life. These examples fill me with hope. Not hope that environmental damage can be averted; it's too late for that. But hope that such damage can be limited and contained during the next few crucial decades, and hope that we can in some measure recover. In travels to urban South America, village India, and the deep forests of the eastern United States, I found proof that there are other, less damaging ways to lead satisfying human lives, evidence that our infatuation with accumulation and expansion is not the only possibility. No trips I've ever taken have thrilled me as much. No previous journeys made the world seem so pliable, the character of human beings so open, the future so uninevitable.

But I hesitate to admit my hope, for the word has been debased— as "hope" is used in the context of the environment, people always seem to hope that the scientists are wrong, hope that their warnings are just "doom and gloom," hope that we'll "muddle through." Such is the message of the currently fashionable crop of "environmental optimists." But that's not hope—that's wishing. Real hope implies real willingness to change, perhaps in some of the directions suggested by this volume. Those suggestions, I repeat, seem out of step with the politics and the economics of the moment. But that does not mean change is impossible; all it means is that our politics is—temporarily— out of step with the chemistry and physics of the earth.

Chapter 1
HOME

On August 15, 1587, Virginia Dare became the first child born to English parents in the New World. Her birthplace—Roanoke Island, in what is now North Carolina—represented Britain's first attempt at colonizing this continent. Though this particular band of settlers did not survive intact, Roanoke Island marks the beginning of the historical process that in the subsequent four centuries saw English-speaking Europeans settle and subdue North America.

On September 14, 1987, 400 years and 29 days later, a team of biologists from the U.S. Fish and Wildlife Service office on Roanoke Island opened the gate of a pen and released a pair of red wolves into the Alligator River National Wildlife Refuge. The animals disappeared into the woods perhaps a half hour's drive from the spot where Dare was born. They were the first animals in the history of the planet ever to have gone extinct in the wild and then, from a remnant population in zoos around the nation, been reintroduced to the natural world. They were, surely as Dare, pioneers.

The forces set in motion by European colonization had all but erased red wolves from the continent: settlers made wolves a symbol of the devil, placed bounties on their heads, organized state and federal predator-control programs, and farmed and developed their last few strongholds. But the Roanoke Island biologists have watched and listened for the last eight years as these radio-collared animals have spread out and reproduced across the refuge's swampy, mosquito-infested 150,000 acres. As of autumn 1994, the biologists had counted sixty-one wild-born puppies. One wild-born female had borne four litters, and one of her pups had in turn given birth— a third generation of wild red wolves howling in the night.

★   ★   ★

Five hundred miles to the north, from his home on Nantucket, plant ecologist Peter Dunwiddie studies core samples of swamps and bogs, looking at pollen under a microscope to figure out what was growing on Cape Cod and the surrounding Atlantic islands in the time before, and after, the Pilgrims debarked in nearby Plymouth. It's easy to spot the onset of European settlement in his pollen samples. "Literally in a matter of decades the forest was cleared— there's no more oak pollen, and all of a sudden lots of grass pollen," says Dunwiddie. "That persisted throughout much of the following couple of hundred years," as Europeans turned most of the area into a giant sheep pasture.

In the late 1800s, just as the agricultural economy was beginning to dwindle, people began taking photographs. And Dunwiddie has gathered, along with his pollen samples, a vast library of original pictures, as well as photos taken from the same places fifty or a hundred years later. "Here's Prospect Hill on Martha's Vineyard in 1906. You can see a stone wall marching up and over the top of the hill in the distance—there's not a tree to be seen. The retake of the photo today is entirely of an oak forest—a mature oak forest. You can't see the stone wall; you can barely make out the contours of the hill at all because of the forest."

The scenario repeats itself all over the area—pitch pine and post oak replacing pasture. "Sometimes we had to use a ladder and a pole to get the camera above the treetops just to take a picture," says Dunwiddie. In his bog cores, too, "the pollen is beginning to resemble the pre-European. The oak and pine pollen is showing up as a real blip right at the top of the sediment." And it will likely continue. Coyotes, which in the 1980s crossed the canal and established themselves on Cape Cod, have recently managed the ocean crossing to the more remote Elizabeth Islands. "They've very quickly decimated all the feral sheep that were left out there," reports Dunwiddie. "They're taking quite a toll on the deer population. The deer and the sheep had been browsing down all the vegetation; there's likely to be a really dramatic spurt of growth."

★   ★   ★

Last spring, on a nice sunny day, a flood of water three feet deep suddenly inundated the road that runs past my door, sweeping whole trees out into the lake. It subsided as suddenly as it had risen; within fifteen minutes the road was drying out. I hiked up the stream down which the flood had come, noting the trunks left on high ground, the channels carved by the rush of water. And half a mile back in the woods I found what I knew I would: a blown-out beaver dam that had released five or six feet of pond with a sudden boom. One mislaid branch, one repair put off too long, some small mistake had finally rewarded the water for its patience. But never mind—what was once pond will soon be a green, rich clearing. And the beavers had already moved a quarter of a mile up the stream, ready to start again their endless alterations to the landscape.

An unremarkable event, in the larger scheme of things, except that a hundred years ago there would have been no beavers here. Like most of the rest of the eastern United States, the Adirondack Mountains, where I live, had been cut over and trapped out. The forests had been overhunted; the streams ran brown with pollution from the mills and tanneries. And now the Adirondacks have recovered: most of the animals that were chased from here have returned, to great tracts of state-protected wilderness.

Which is to say, I live surrounded by contradiction. Six years ago I wrote a book called *The End of Nature*. It argued that human beings were ending the very idea of wildness—that as our cars, factories, and burning forests filled the skies with greenhouse gases, we had finally become large enough to alter the most basic vital sign of the planet, its climate. As we heated the planet, I said, we would change the flora and the fauna *everywhere*; even at the poles or in the Adirondack wilderness, we now influenced every physical system.

The intervening years have made this argument surer. Only the outermost fringe of scientists now doubt the reality and power of global warming and other large-scale environmental damage. Since the book was published we have experienced the warmest year in recorded history, a small taste of what the climate-scientists say is in store for us. For the first time humans are altering the most fundamental phenomena. We have grown so big that we literally overshadow the earth. Nature as something separate from man has vanished.

Writing that book depressed me, and many of its readers both here and abroad have told me that they were depressed as well. Which is appropriate: it should depress us to live on a planet that becomes less complex and wild with each passing day, and it should depress us even more that we are the cause of that change. Most of this book is devoted to strategies for retooling our societies and economies so they do less damage: that is the hard and unending work that will occupy us throughout our lifetime. It is the particular challenge that history presents those of us who happen to be alive at the moment. If we can't prevent the environmental damage already underway, we can—if we act boldly—limit it. But I no longer think fear is sufficient motivation to make such changes, especially since they involve the most fundamental aspects of our economies, our societies, and our individual lives. To spur us on we need hope as well—we need a vision of recovery, of renewal, of resurgence.

Which is why this book begins where it begins—why it begins, in a sense, with dessert. For as it happens, I live surrounded each day by one form of that splendid new vision. I live on the East Coast of the United States.

★   ★   ★

Imagine the view from a satellite, writes Alan Durning in the 1994 edition of the Worldwatch Institute's *State of the World* report. A time-lapse film that showed you a thousand years each minute would reveal only the slightest changes in the earth's forests: millennia upon millennia, they covered about a third of the planet's land surface.

But in the film's last three seconds, the years since 1950,

> the change accelerates explosively. Vast tracts of forest vanish from Japan, the Philippines, and the mainland of Southeast Asia, from most of Central America and the horn of Africa, from western North America and eastern South America, from the Indian subcontinent and sub-Saharan Africa . . . Southeast Asia resembles a dog with the mange. Malaysian Borneo is shaved. In the final fractions of a second, the clearing spreads to Siberia and the Canadian north. Forests disappear so suddenly from so many places that it looks like a plague of locusts has descended on the planet.

If you stared from outer space at the rural stretches of eastern North America, however, you'd see something different—a patch of green spreading like mold across bread. Spreading fast. In the early nineteenth century, Timothy Dwight, a Boston cleric, reported that a 240-mile journey from his home to New York City passed no more than twenty miles of forest; surveying the changes wrought by farmers and loggers in New Hampshire he wrote: "The forests are not only cut down, but there appears little reason to hope they will ever grow again."

Less than two centuries later, and despite great increases in population, 90 percent of New Hampshire is covered by forest. Vermont has gone from 35 percent woods in 1850 to 80 percent today, and even Massachusetts has seen its woodlands rebound to the point where they cover nearly two-thirds of the commonwealth. This process, which began as the fertile fields of the Midwest replaced the cold and rocky pastures of the East, has not yet run its course; forest cover in New York State, for instance, continued to grow by more than a million acres a decade through 1980. In sum, says Douglas MacCleery of the U.S. Department of Agriculture, "the forest and farmland landscape of the Appalachians, as well as many other parts of the East and South, has come full circle. By the 1960s and 1970s, the pattern of forest, field, and pasture was similar to that prior to 1800, its appearance much like it must have been prior to the American Revolution."

If you're looking for hope, this unintentional and mostly unnoticed renewal represents the great environmental story of the United States—in some ways, of the whole world. Here, not far from where "suburb" and "megalopolis" were added to the world's vocabulary, an explosion of green is under way. In the therapeutic terms of the moment, this is the first region on earth to hit bottom and then, blessed with adequate rainfall, go into recovery. In his journal Thoreau listed the species gone from Concord by the middle of the nineteenth century: bear, moose, deer, porcupine, wolf, beaver, turkey. In 1989 environmental police had to kill a moose that had taken up residence on the median strip of Route 128, "America's Computer Highway," near Concord. "We've never been faced with a moose ten miles from Boston," said one game warden, who donated the animal's carcass to a Salvation Army soup kitchen. Further north, 316 moose were killed in collisions with cars in 1987 in Maine—in a state where, according to one eighteenth-century historian, "it is rare to see one at the present time." The same stories can be told about deer (there was no deer season in Vermont from 1865 to 1897, because there were no deer) or beaver or coyote or bear. "The shad, the eagle, and the turkey are returning," a team of Abenaki Indians wrote recently in a book about the northern forest. "The bear, the moose, and many of our other relations have shown us the ways of life, and have taught us and sustained us. Their life and our life are one." Present tense.

American heads jerk to the west when we think about nature—the splendor of the Rockies and the Sierras and the red rock desert captivates us all. And yet nature in the East is every bit as real and profound, imbued with its own mythos. We should take as our emblem the pine—not the towering King's Arrow pines marked by the first lumbermen for the Royal Navy, but the spindly pines that spring up when the cows leave a pasture, that begin the long process of reclamation. Our boast should not be of our history, but of our future—of the someday old growth now consolidating its hold on ridge after hill after valley bottom. From the Pisgahs, the Unakas, the Nantahalas of the southern Appalachians, to the Whites and Greens and Adirondacks of the North, these mountains and woods are coming back—and people are starting to notice. In the late 1980s Congress passed the Northern Forest Lands Council Act, calling for a study on how to protect the forests of New York, New Hampshire, Vermont, and Maine—forests that in some cases weren't there a hundred years ago. "Show me another twenty-six-million-acre chunk," says John Harrigan, a New Hampshire newspaper editor who sat on the study commission. "Outside of Seward's Folly, I don't think you can." Yellowstone Park, by contrast, covers 2 million acres.

So I want to tell this story of hope. Not because the East is a paradise now, but precisely because it isn't. Our woods will never again be forest primeval: they will forever be affected by our economies and habits, by our care or carelessness. Wilderness—in its truest sense, of places totally separated from human influence—is extinguished, here as everywhere else. But I'm done mourning. Innocence gone, we need to work wisely to build societies that allow natural recovery, that let the rest of creation begin, however tentatively, to flourish once more. And we need to do it quickly, for the recovery even of the East is tentative and uncertain. Every kind of human threat imperils this new nature, as we shall soon see. For the moment, though, I want this region to stand for the most bottom-line kind of hope; as I tell its story, imagine what could happen to your own place, wherever it is, if people backed off a little.

Nature's grace in the American East offers this hope to a world in terrible need of models. For the East is a typical place—a place where large populations live in and around the recovering woods and rivers. In that way, it looks like the rest of the world—like Siberia and the vast stretches of forested Asia, like Central and South America, like Africa. In place of the increasingly sterile debate between wilderness and civilization, between raped and virgin, it offers at least the outside possibility of marriage. And it is real, too, because of the devastation it has undergone, a devastation now sweeping the rest of the world. In Haiti, forest cover has dropped from 80 percent to 5 percent; in parts of the Philippines, a "chainsaw massacre of the regal hardwoods" has left erosion, silted streams, and "weather veering from drought to flood." The same was true of much of Appalachia a century ago; though other climates and soils may offer even greater challenges, the resurgence of forest here gives some distant promise that in other places in future days people may once again be able to rely on a replenished and revivified nature to provide them with a modest and reliable life. "What an incredibly short cycle it's been in the East," said Peter Dunwiddie as we walked one day through a tiny patch of surviving old growth in Maine's

North Woods. "Maybe it's a good sign for places like Rondonia in the Amazon."

At the very least, it's a poetic sign. Here, where a certain kind of exploitation began, the fever has largely run its course. That fever still ravages most of the rest of the world, and indeed it finds much of its direction and its capital in the financial and political centers of the American East. But a little way away, outside the cities and suburbs, the ghost map of this place is reasserting itself: the bear and the turkey and the moose reclaiming their place, the trees growing up around the million stone walls. The old frontiers have closed; that, we are told, is the story of American history and indeed of world history. But a new frontier may be opening here—an expanding frontier of recovery that, given infinite human care and nurturing, might follow the waves of destruction across the continent and then around the world. On a hill in coastal Maine, the body of naturalist author Henry Beston is buried on the edge of a second-growth pine forest. His epitaph is from his classic book about Cape Cod, *The Outermost House:* "Creation is still going on, the creative forces are as great and as active today as they have ever been, and tomorrow's morning will be as heroic as any of the world." We have little choice in this hard-pinched world but to hope that he was right; and the region where he lived his life offers us at least the slender chance that it is so.

*   *   *

The story of this recovery, a story that must be told in its detail to have any meaning, properly begins long before man arrived on this shore. It is worth remembering that no spot on the globe was originally more natural or wild than any other—over deep time eastern mountains have risen to heights we would now consider western, been eroded, and risen again. The rock on Grandfather Mountain in western North Carolina, rising four thousand feet above the Piedmont Plain, is over a billion years old, among the oldest on the planet.

And in the southern stretches of the mountain East, biological time is nearly as unfathomable as the geologic. Along the Blue Ridge and its surrounding highlands, neither glacier nor ocean has covered the land for hundreds of millions of years, thereby creating a rare biological refuge that preserves much of the story of evolution. Plants could travel slowly north and south along the ridges of the Appalachians as climates changed, escaping extinction. Consequently, the Smokies boast 1,400 flowering plants and a hundred types of trees. Arguably they form the most diverse temperate forest in the world. Biologists have counted, along with the flowers and trees, 350 mosses and liverworts, 230 lichens, and perhaps 2,000 types of fungi. The Smokies are also home to 23 species of snake, not to mention the salamander capital of the nation, with at least 39 species. The mountains look soft and rounded in the gentle Carolina mist, but their wet warmth means an understory of mountain laurel and rhododendron dense enough to make bushwhacking an almost Amazonian experience.

Farther north, time is much more recent. Eleven thousand years ago glaciers covered the northern forest of New England and New York with a mile of ice. On their retreat the rock and till were colonized by fungi and lichens adapted to the cold, converting the rock to soil that would make a home for the forests that were migrating north from their southern retreats. But never an easy home—

though warm air from the Midwest and the Gulf and cold fronts from Canada mean abundant precipitation through the seasons, the soil is not deep. Highly acidic and fragile, it barely allows agriculture; the short growing seasons have favored spruce and fir forests on the northern edges, and a mix of maple, beech, and birch in slightly warmer sections.

Altogether, about three-quarters of America's original forest was found in the eastern third of the nation—and about three-quarters of the nation's forest today is in the East. Most of it, of course, is not the same forest. When you see the remnant slivers of old-growth woods that are still left in the East, you begin to viscerally understand why some westerners are battling so hard to save their larger virgin stands. I paddled one day down the Black River in North Carolina, a lazy stretch of water not far from Cape Fear, where through a series of flukes, loggers bypassed an extensive stand of bald cypress. David Stahle and Malcolm Cleaveland, University of Arkansas climate researchers looking for trees to core in order to establish historical rainfall patterns, "discovered" the trees in the mid-1980s. The first tree they cored was eight hundred years old, and soon they'd come across others that were at least seventeen hundred years old. "One of the traits of these trees is hollowness in the core—there's no question in my mind they're two thousand years old," says Stahle. That is to say, they are the oldest living things east of Nevada's ancient bristlecone pines. Now preserved by the Nature Conservancy, the river is a kind of Pleistocene Park. Resurrection fern grows from crooks in the ancient trunks, and Spanish moss hangs in the humid air; white ibis float overhead, and prothonotary warblers sound in the hollows. To germinate, the trees need dry ground but afterward grow in water, so it takes a hurricane that clears the canopy, followed by a four- or five-year drought, for a new tree to get established. That might happen every four or five centuries—time seems immaterial among the cypresses.

Most of the forests of the East, though, are haunted by time. By the human history that brings time into being, a human history that long predates Columbus. Paleo-Indians moved into the northern forest area not long after the glaciers receded; some recent evidence indicates, in fact, that the earliest pioneers crossed the land bridge with Asia and came straight east across the continent before they spread out across the West. Scientists continue to debate whether these first arrivals were the cause of the sudden dying-off of megafauna that once roamed the East: the mammoths and mastodons, camels and ground sloths, giant beavers and armadillos, the dire wolf and the saber-toothed tiger. There is no question, however, that over thousands of years Indians rearranged the landscape to suit their needs. "It is tempting to believe that when the Europeans arrived in the New World they confronted Virgin Lands, the Forest Primeval, a wilderness which had existed for eons uninfluenced by human hands," writes William Cronon in his masterful account of New England's early history, *Changes in the Land*. "Nothing could be further from the truth." Indians cleared land for agriculture and burned some forests once or twice a year, keeping them open and parklike.

But the Indian disruptions, though extensive, tended to be temporary—the annual fires, for instance, spread quickly and, because there was little accumulated underbrush, rarely grew out of control. And since the Indians were unencumbered by European notions of property, when they had used one area for a time they often moved to another. Not so the whites who followed: "New England lumbering used forests as if they would last forever," writes Cronon. The tall white pines were cut first, destined to be made into masts. The white cedar went next—and neither tree tends to regrow, so the feel of the forest began to change as more deciduous trees sprang up. Across much of the East, though, the logger was not as destructive as the farmers who followed. They removed *every* tree as they cleared their fields, turning the logs into fences—fences that enclosed the livestock which Cronon calls "the single most distinguishing characteristic of European agricultural practices." Everything changed with animals that spent the year in a single place, eating constantly—even the grass on the ground. Native grasses had not evolved to pasture cows; they were soon overwhelmed by exotics that arrived in shipboard fodder, including new weeds such as mulleins, mallows, nightshades, stinging nettles, and dandelions. Other agricultural techniques left their own devastation. Instead of rotating crops, farmers tended to plant corn year after year; and corn, of course, is a heavy feeder and exhausts the soil quickly. Colonial farmers often used fish as fertilizer—in some places a dollar would buy you a thousand fish, says Cronon. The colonial squandering of resources is best typified, perhaps, by the use of firewood to heat homes. Open fireplaces in almost every room of a house kept homes hot through the winter; they also consumed, on average, more than thirty cords of wood a year, or about an acre of forest.

The exploitation of the coastal areas where colonists first landed was merely a warm-up, however, for the destruction that accelerated in the eighteenth and nineteenth centuries as populations grew and the nation industrialized. Between 1785 and 1850 the population of the United States grew nearly eightfold, from 3 million to nearly 2.3 million people. It took about three acres of cropland to feed each one; so by 1850, says forest researcher Douglas MacCleery, total land in grain and vegetables had grown to 76 million acres, a number that quadrupled to 319 million acres by 1900. For a while the trees that farmers cleared away for fields met the nation's demand for timber, but in the second half of the nineteenth century lumber consumption rose from 5.4 billion board feet a year to 44.5 billion board feet. Wood was used for *everything*; it was the cornerstone of the economy in the same way petroleum and its byproducts are today. Even iron was smelted using wood charcoal: a thousand-ton ironworks needed twenty or thirty thousand acres of forest to sustain itself, according to MacCleery. A square forty-acre field required eight thousand fence rails—by 1850, when barbed wire began to replace wood, there were 3.2 million miles of wooden fence in America. The wood freed up by wire fencing was soon claimed by the expanding railroads, whose demand for cars, ties, fuel, bridges, trestles, stations, and telegraph poles was taking a quarter of the nation's timber by the turn of the century. Each mile of track needed twenty-five hundred crossties, and since they weren't treated with preservative, they had to be replaced every five or six years; ties alone took between 15 and 20 million acres of American forest by 1900. Steamboats burned wood for fuel until the Civil War—they consumed a fifth of all the fuelwood sold in 1840.

These were the years of the greatest logging drives, the years when whole states were deforested by crosscut saws and teams of horses. In the last half of the nineteenth century, forest cover in much of the East had fallen from 70 percent to 20 percent or less. And people noticed the effects. The lessons were perhaps most obvious in New England, where the destruction had first begun. Snow melted earlier in deforested areas and ran off more quickly without roots to soak it up. Mills found themselves flooded in springtime and high and dry by midsummer. Great forest fires, many set by errant sparks from logging railroads, claimed hundreds of thousands of acres. Erosion increased dramatically—Cronon cites evidence that ponds and lakes were filling in five times as fast as before Europeans had arrived. The denuded forests, the drained swamps, the exhausted fields gave rise, in fact, to the first great work of modern environmentalism, George Perkins Marsh's *Man and Nature*. "We are breaking up the floor and wainscotting and doors and window-frames of our dwelling for fuel to warm our bodies," Marsh warned.

But when the fever broke, only rarely was it because of the warnings of men like Marsh. Mostly, the devastation of eastern forests was driven by economics—just as today the devastation of the Amazon or Irian Jaya is driven by economics—and when the economics changed, so did the look of the land. Sometimes new technology helped: eight hundred patents were issued before the Civil War for more efficient stove designs, more than for any other product. Coal and oil began to replace wood as a fuel source in the late nineteenth century. Wood provided 90 percent of America's energy in 1850, a figure that fell to 10 percent by 1920. (Though even the move to coal required massive amounts of wood for the millions upon millions of mine props.) Meanwhile, the profligate cutting left lumbermen little choice but to move on west: there were no mature forests left to take. From New England to New York, Pennsylvania, the Great Lakes, and the South the loggers moved; lumber production in the South finally peaked in 1909.

Something similar was happening in agriculture. Even where lands had not been exhausted by poor farming, improved transportation to the fertile soils of the Midwest meant insurmountable competition. The opening of the Erie Canal in 1825 is as good a starting point as any. In the decades that followed, the Northeast stopped concentrating on raw materials and began the long transition to manufacturing and service economies. Take Vermont as an example. The first merino sheep had arrived near Mount Ascutney in 1809. By 1840 there were 1,681,000 of them in the state, or six per person. Thirty years later that number had been cut in half: the western ranches could ship their wool by rail and undercut the Vermonters. The dairy industry survived much longer, milk being harder to transport, but it, too, has been in long decline. By 1890, 42 percent of the people born in Vermont lived elsewhere. It was a Vermont native, Horace Greeley, who is supposed to have said "Go West, young man." Among those who took his advice was John Deere, whose machinery would transform the plains. According to author Ben Bachman, Vermont alone produced 35 U.S. senators, 114 congressmen, and 60 governors who served in other states. "Vermont recovered because the destruction was a one-shot destruction," says Steve Trombulak, a Middlebury College biologist. "It was cleared, pastured for maybe twenty or thirty years, and then everyone discovered Ohio. I don't believe for a moment that Vermont would look like this if it wasn't for the Louisiana Purchase. If we hadn't found places where you didn't break your plow on the stones."

Government at most ratified the individual decisions of millions of small farmers and loggers. The 1911 passage of the Weeks Act stands as a kind of coda to this wave of exploitation; it allowed Washington to acquire national forest lands in the East, largely to protect the watersheds of navigable streams. The first acquisitions came in the southern Appalachians and the White Mountains of New Hampshire; by World War II, when the federal government pretty much stopped buying land, the Forest Service owned

Forest Service owned

24 million acres of "depleted farmsteads and cutover and burned woodlands." Unlike the West, where the Forest Service soon busied itself learning how to cut down its holdings, it didn't do much with its eastern lands. They were simply too degraded; they needed time to recover.

The twentieth century has been that time. The coastlines, of course, have boomed, as suburbs sprawled out from the cities in ever more wasteful rings. But inland, first in the North and then in the Southeast, the number of acres of forest was soon on the increase. The relaxation of the land is more widespread than most imagine. We think of Ohio as classic Midwest, but the southern part of the state, where Kentucky and West Virginia abut, was the center of one of the richest forests on earth. In 1805 the French botanist François André Michaux wrote that "in more than a thousand leagues of the country over which I have traveled at different times in North America, I do not remember having seen one to compare with the Ohio Valley for the vegetative strength of its forests." Hard hit by logging, coal mining, and marginal farming, the forests declined. But then the population shrunk as those industries failed, and the forests began to grow back. "It's the center of one of the great biomes on earth, and there's been some recovery," says Reed Noss, the editor of *Conservation Biology*, who has worked on preservation plans for the region. An Ohio State University professor using satellite data and ground maps recently compared the region as it was in 1938 with that of 1988. He found that fifty years ago there were 2,146 "polygons"—farm fields, clearcuts, and other definable boundaries. In 1988 the number was down to 710—the woods were reclaiming pasture and road. "What's gone on in this landscape is revegetation," he says. Go a little farther west in Ohio, though, and the woods have not grown back. Clark County, say, was a third forested in 1805, 91 percent farmland in 1891, and 93 percent farmland in 1993. You can almost define the division between East and Midwest by looking for the places where trees have returned.

If you walk in the woods, you can see the process up close—see the cellar holes now sprouting birch, see the careful piles of stone now covered by moss and surrounded by forest. In the Cattaloochee district of the Great Smoky Mountains National Park, where 765 people lived in 1906 and logged the slopes intensively (and where the Cherokees once fished and hunted and burned for game), old doorframes still stand in what is now deep forest. It looks halfway to ancient, this forest—it's hard to imagine that it was cleared land in this century. You can see the process along the rivers and creeks of the region, where hundreds of old dams have washed out over the years and have never been replaced. From the window where I type these words, I can see the crumbling stone dam that powered a small Adirondack sawmill that once skimmed the trees from all the surrounding ridges. Trees gone; sawmill gone. Sawmill gone; trees return.

These words may sound heartless. The people who cleared this land worked hard, harder than I've ever worked. They dreamed good dreams, built good lives, mostly lived ethically and responsibly by the values and the beliefs of their day. They wasted less than I do; their environmental impact, in some global sense, was incomparably smaller than mine. Neither do I mean to suggest that the forests that recovered as they moved west are the same forests that they found—massive human intervention cannot be shrugged off by a few decades of salutary neglect. Biologist Trombulak talks about dozens of species that may have gone extinct in the Northeast, most because they depended on the old-growth forest; whatever our spotted owls were, we lost them two centuries ago. It is a different place than it was, in ways subtle and large. There were no daisies before the Europeans came, and no dandelions.

And yet for me the proof that what is happening is significant— and right and necessary—lies in the recovery not only of the forests themselves, but of much of the life they always supported. The best measure of our willingness as a species to accept some limits is the ability of the rest of creation to find space enough around us to pursue its own destiny. And in the rural East, wildlife has been recovering at a giddy pace.

As early as 1672 wild turkey were described as rare in Massachusetts; a century later they were such relics of history that a popular farmer's manual described the bird as "a large domestick fowl, brought from Turkey." Beaver were disappearing from the Massachusetts coast as early as 1640, and from the Narragansett region by 1660, as Indians and others filled the demands of the fur-trading posts that had to keep moving farther up the rivers. Massachusetts had its first closed season on deer in 1694; Cronon quotes Timothy Dwight, the Boston cleric of the early nineteenth century: "Hunting with us exists chiefly in tales of other times."

But just as the last animals were vanishing, organized sportsmen's groups, led by men like Theodore Roosevelt, banded together to oppose market hunting, enact game laws, and establish refuges and reserves. Their efforts meshed with the slow return of habitat, and numbers boomed. Whitetail deer now number 18 million, perhaps half the original size of the herd but forty times larger than the number in the late 1800s. Pennsylvania motorists alone killed forty-three thousand deer in 1990, and the animals browse so much suburban shrubbery that some call them "rats with hooves." An esti-mated forty thousand black bears roam the East; John McPhee has written extensively, including an essay called "A Textbook Place for Bears," on their return to New Jersey and Pennsylvania. Alligators, placed on the endangered species list in 1967 after hunting had nearly wiped them out, rebounded within ten years to a population of 2 million. In 1972 thirty-seven wild turkeys were introduced to western Massachusetts—by now the population tops ten thousand.

I have an extensive collection of newspaper clippings about moose. "Rude Moose Hauled from Mainer's Pool," for instance, tells of an eight-hundred-pound bull moose that, twice in the same week, had to be dragged from a swimming pool in Lewiston, Maine's second-largest city. Next to a picture of a yearling moose in an upstate New York paper: "Name that moose! A yearling moose is wander-ing around Saratoga County, having been seen in several places near the Northway. Help us name her. The best suggestion from a reader will win a Bullwinkle hat or video." Not all the stories are so funny: as many as six hundred Maine moose a year are killed by cars. (Since moose are so tall, their eyes don't shine in headlights, and many driv-ers don't see them till they come through the windshield.) But their presence and the boom in their numbers, even after the renewal of hunting seasons in New England—shows that the swampy spruce and fir forests of the North are intact enough to support their num-bers. In fact, the spread of the moose has led some to call for the reintroduction of elk and bison, both of which roamed the East in large numbers. (Ask yourself why Buffalo is named Buffalo.) Elk used to migrate in herds, from New York down what we now know as Interstate 81 to Tennessee and Kentucky. The last Pennsylvania elk was killed in the fall of 1867, but a small herd reintroduced from

Yellowstone in the 1920s has grown to more than two hundred animals today; and the state helps farmers pay for electric fencing to keep the elk out of cornfields.

As game have spread, so have predators. The most fearsome are probably family dogs, capable of killing huge quantities of deer for sheer sport. But their cousins, the coyotes, have also appeared in large numbers, perhaps moving in from the West to partially fill the niche once held by timber wolves; even in heavily settled Massachusetts, coyotes unknown till the late 1950s—now live in virtually every Bay State town.

Larger predators may also be returning to the eastern forest. In rural uplands throughout the region, that part of the imagination elsewhere reserved for Elvis sightings is given over to stories about panthers, cougars, pumas, mountain lions, catamounts. Officially, there aren't any of these long-tailed cats. As the final clearing of the region took place in the nineteenth century, and as the deer herds that were their prey base vanished, cougars were wiped out across the East. The catamount is Vermont's mascot, but the last one was killed in November 1881.

The Maryland-based Eastern Puma Research Network, however, reports eighteen hundred sightings in the last decade; and just last year Vermont game officials confirmed that they had found cougar scat near Craftsbury. (Cougars groom themselves constantly with their tongues; scat with cougar hair, therefore, comes from cougars.) The year before, during deer season, a Maine hunter heard a sound "like a woman screaming in pain." Topping a rise he saw a large, tawny animal shaking something in its mouth. The animal turned toward him, and he saw a "big angry head—about the size of an average human head." It snarled, dropped its prey, and disappeared in "three tremendous long leaps." The hunter collected the carcass of the prey, which turned out to be a bobcat—a smaller feline more common in the northern forest. The biologists said the bite and claw marks on the bobcat were the right size and shape for a cougar. It is a different woods with a mountain lion in it. The sightings increase each year; the wildness seems to gather.

★   ★   ★

The restored wildness of the East, its renewed vigor, seems to concentrate most purely in one patch of the region: my patch, the Adirondack Park of upstate New York. New York, of course, can boast like few other states—capital of world politics, linchpin of world finance, incandescent hub of art and drama. And yet greater than all of these may be the little-known legacy of the Adirondacks, the world's first experiment in restoring an entire ecosystem.

The Adirondacks cover one quarter of New York State. They are bigger than Vermont or New Hampshire; bigger than Yellowstone, Yosemite, Glacier, and Grand Canyon National Parks combined. People came late to this rugged landscape. Even the Indians used much of the land solely as a seasonal hunting area. High, harsh, and cold, its loftiest peak had not been climbed by a white man until decades after Lewis and Clark returned from the Pacific. But when people finally arrived, they did so with a vengeance—loggers, especially, penetrated the very heart of the mountains, searching after pine and then spruce and then whatever. My township was devastated by the tanneries, which cut down hemlocks by the millions to use the bark for curing hides and then poisoned the rivers with the runoff. Elsewhere, the loggers came after saw timber or pulp—the first images of clearcut devastation that Americans ever saw were magazine drawings of the Adirondack streams from the late 1800s.

The horse teams and crosscut saws, the farmers and the trappers, managed to chase off most of the wildlife. They left behind just a few stands of old-growth forest—a hundred thousand acres, perhaps, in the Five Ponds wilderness in the northeastern corner of the park, along with many smaller patches scattered throughout the mountains. It is splendid to walk in these timeless forests—spruces a hundred feet high, yellow birch and hemlock a dozen feet around at the base, moss-crumbled nurse logs scattered on the forest floor.

But ancient forest is not the real glory of the Adirondacks. It's the new forest merging with the old, the groves thirty and fifty and a hundred years old that are increasingly indistinguishable from old growth. New old growth. Perhaps no place on the planet has recovered as comprehensively from deforestation as these mountains five hours' drive from New York City. The Adirondacks are the Yellowstone of rebirth, the Yosemite of revival, the second-chance Alaska. For conservationists imagining not simply the salvation of what remains pristine, but the restoration of what has been degraded, this is just about the most heartening spot on earth. The Adirondacks offer a few scattered reminders of what Eden looked like, and a million vistas from which to imagine redemption.

Some of the recovery has been purely accidental. In a land where the growing season runs ninety days in a good year, and the first thirty of those are spent swatting black flies, only one generation of farmers tried to cultivate the cleared lands. But much of the credit for the health of these mountains belongs with human beings—with the people of New York who, seventy five years before politicians anywhere else discovered "ecology," began the process of protecting these hills. Early visitors (the world's first ecotourists, swells from the city who journeyed north for the wilderness and soon built great camps and hotels) were appalled by the rate at which the trees were falling; their concern merged with the more hardheaded worries of the state's industrialists that the Hudson would begin to silt up as whole mountains eroded and that the waterways which were the state's economic lifelines would deteriorate. These two factions combined in the state legislature to produce landmark legislation setting up a forest preserve and, in the summer of 1894, declaring that it "shall be forever kept as wild forest lands. [It] shall not be leased, sold, or exchanged, or be taken by any corporation, public or private, nor shall the timber thereon be sold, removed, or destroyed."

The state did not buy every inch of these mountains. It acquired land slowly but steadily, often when timber barons couldn't pay their taxes: by the 1990s, about 42 percent of the park was actually in public hands. And it is these "forever wild" lands that have served as the backbone of the recovery. Two-thirds of the land in the town where I live belongs to the state of New York. If you walk west from my back door, you hit state land in minutes and can continue on it for days.

If you did so, your trip would be glorious in its ordinariness. Almost everywhere in America we have saved the grand rocks and ice; in the Adirondacks, too, the sheer granite of the High Peaks is well protected and well hiked, some of the trails rutted so deeply you nearly disappear from view. But the High Peaks are barely a sixth of the park. The rest is the kind of land that in so many other spots has been cut, drained, filled, and developed. Not sheer cliffs, but swamp and spruce thicket and mile upon mile of hardwood and hemlock. You reach pond after pond called "Mud" or "Round" or "Fish" or "Second" or "Thirteenth." There are thousands upon thousands of mountains too short to be bare on top, never climbed by people because there's no reason, except maybe venison, to climb them. If you do stumble to the top, instead of sweeping views you get strained glimpses through the lattice of bare branches. If you find a fire scar or other small opening, the vista is of six or seven or eight or nine lines of ridge, all rounded and soft in the twilight. This place was saved for ecological reasons; it is the nearest we have to an intact ecosystem. Gazing out over it gives me a primeval thrill even more powerful than the view from the top of Mount Rainier or El Capitan: *so this is what the world looked like.*

And could look like again—for a very different Adirondacks are easily remembered by the oldest residents. Crow Mountain, in whose shadow I live, offers a 360-degree view of unbroken forest, save for a few roads and houses and the spire of the Methodist church. "I remember when you could hardly see a tree from the top," one of my neighbors says with some regret, for he recalls as well the agricultural community that existed ("flourished" would be much too strong a word) here in his youth. But the small dairies have closed, and their pasture reverted first to pine and birch and now to the trailing species, the beeches and the hemlocks and the maples that dominate our forest once again.

With the woods have come the critters that once lived in them. Just as in other areas across the East, there's been a slow but steady progression of animals back to the burrows and dens of their ancestors. Fifty years ago much local excitement attended the first bear seen in town in living memory; now bears seem as obvious a part of the landscape as trees, their berry-dyed scat and their nighttime hooting a common part of life. A decade ago it was the return of wild turkeys that dominated talk at the barbershop; now they, too, are common. Otter swim in the rivers and ponds; fisher and marten have long since rebounded.

At the moment, we are all worked up over moose. The animals reappeared in the Adirondacks in the 1980s, having wandered over from their increasingly crowded homes in Maine, New Hampshire, and Vermont. Some New York conservationists wanted to "reintroduce" them, trucking more moose over to swell the new herd. Most locals—already a little worried about colliding with one-ton ungulates on back roads—argued convincingly that moose were returning on their own, and that the $2 million budget for the project might be put to better use. And indeed the moose have kept right on multiplying. There was one on our creek last week; word soon spread throughout the area, the same peal of exhilaration that greeted the bear two generations ago and that I pray will greet the wolf in my daughter's day.

To me, though, the greatest of all the returned exiles is that large and bucktoothed rodent, the beaver. Once all but wiped out by trappers—its habitat eroded by drying streams—the beaver has rebounded with such vigor that there may not be a stream in the Adirondacks without a lodge: floods like the one described at the beginning of this chapter are commonplace. For years now beaver have had a big dam right next to our house. Our only neighbors—summer people who show up for a weekend every month or two—try to knock the dam down, working hard to dismantle the carefully placed sticks and logs. Within a night, however, the hole is plugged. The trees have died in the new wetlands behind the dam, and its murky, slimy waters are filled with all the many forms of life that thrive in murk and slime. It hums, vibrates with frog and insect. Soon—next year, maybe, since they're running out of accessible trees—the beavers will move on down the stream and make themselves a new pond. Slowly the dam will give way and the water leak out; then the pond will grow into a meadow, and the trees begin to take over once more—shouldering slowly in toward the center like schoolboys around a fistfight. I can take you to a hundred places within walking distance where this transformation is happening. *On some Adirondack creeks, man is no longer the chief agent of disturbance and change.* The stream by my home on which the beavers have built their dam was originally called "Beaver Brook." Its name soon changed to Mill Creek, since it was lined for a brief pulse of history with sawmills, gristmills, even a calico mill. The mills have long since closed, though, and the beaver has returned; the old name makes more sense again.

And that sweet thought triggers another, which is at the center of this book. In the Adirondacks, and to a lesser extent throughout the rest of the rural East, we have been given a second chance. This reborn wildness is not all that it once was, and we must operate within certain limits—most notably our large population—not faced by the first Europeans to reach this area. But this second-chance world is not completely broken, either; though its soils and forests have been altered by past human practices, though its climate and weather are now influenced by our gaseous contribution to the atmosphere, it still retains sufficient vigor to reassert itself—for its original species to press up through the weight of our settlement and reestablish themselves. "Though we have caused the earth to be seriously diseased, it is not yet without health," writes Kentucky farmer and essayist Wendell Berry. "The earth we have before us now is still abounding and beautiful. . . . The health of nature is the primary ground of hope—if we can find the humility and wisdom to accept nature as our teacher."

So far we can claim neither humility nor wisdom; our good fortune is mostly accidental, and as we shall see, new dangers born of human carelessness and selfishness threaten even the tentative recovery of this place. Still, the hope represented by the East is real. It is transferable, too, to any other place that still has some open space and some rainfall: surely people on every continent can look at it as a hint of the grace of nature if people back off, give it some room and some time. The world, conceivably, will meet us halfway; the alternative to Eden is not damnation.

★   ★   ★

The problem, of course, is learning to meet the world halfway. So far we show little ability to retreat even a little, to imagine any alternative to the apparently biological imperative to grow and expand. This book is an attempt to prove that this imperative is not in fact biological, that people can figure out other ways to organize their lives. But any such attempt must begin with a frank admission: in most places in the world, human influence is still growing. The eastern United States is at present a bizarre exception—and even its recovery is imperiled.

At the beginning of this century, a quarter of the trees in the eastern forest were American chestnuts. "No other tree grows so rapidly or to such great size on the gravelly hills of the northeastern states," Harvard botanist Charles S. Sargent wrote in his 1890 text, *Silva of North America*. "In early summer, long after the flower of its companions has disappeared, the chestnut covers itself with great masses of spikes of yellow flowers and is then the most magnificent object of the sylvan landscape." In the warm, moist coves of the Smokies, chestnuts grew to twenty feet around; their nuts, once the food of choice for the sky-darkening flocks of passenger pigeons, also supported deer, elk, bear, raccoon, and squirrel, which in turn provided for the predators.

In the first decade of this century, a blight arrived from Europe; within fifty years 80 percent of the chestnuts were dead. Though there are virtually no chestnut trees still standing, *Castanea dentata* is not extinct. New saplings sprout continually from the old trunks. For a time they seem to be healthy—but as soon as they begin to gain any size, they succumb to the blight.

Those saplings provide an appropriate metaphor for the East, and for most of the other scattered and tentative recoveries on this planet. It is true that the Appalachians have begun to repair themselves. But there are blights new and old that may arrest or even reverse the recovery now underway. In particular, the East faces the rebirth of rapacious logging and the push of so-called development, which together may abort this recovery before it grows much stronger, before it can become any kind of beacon to other places. And these economic forces can be seen, in one manifestation or another, all over the world.

And so my emphasis must shift; the rapture be set aside. No more epiphanies about mountain lions and beavers, only the hard work of trying to figure out how that glory might be maintained and even spread. Having admired the chestnut, we need to look long and hard at the blight.

★   ★   ★

Not long ago, on a gorgeous summer day, I climbed into a single-engine Cessna on a small airstrip in northern New Hampshire. The pilot, Rudy Engholm, was the northeastern coordinator of the Environmental Air Force; the other passengers were local environmentalists determined to show me what the North Woods of Vermont, New Hampshire, and especially Maine look like from the air.

The largest green blob on the map of the East, the 10 million acres of the core Maine forest, houses virtually no permanent inhabitants. Loggers go there, as do hunters and fishermen who pay the fees required by the enormous timber companies that own the whole spread. People routinely mistake its emptiness for wildness, but in fact the Maine woods produce huge quantities of pulp for paper, and export whole forests of raw logs to foreign countries. The cutting has been most Bunyanesque in the last fifteen years, as the timber companies have scrambled to "salvage" timber from a spruce budworm infestation.

The damage inflicted on the woods by cutting at this rate is a sight to behold; but you can behold it only by peeking over the narrow "beauty strips" that protect rivers and streams but that also shield passersby from the view of the desert beyond. Hence, our flight. We flew across Lake Umbagog and into Maine, flying for hours over land that knows no human settlement and yet is devastated in ways inconceivable in many more-densely settled parts of the Northeast.

We could see the occasional moose standing on a logging road, but mostly the view was of clearcuts—tracts sometimes thousands of acres in size where every tree was gone. Other spots had been spared clearcutting but had been "high-graded" so relentlessly, with almost every big tree removed, that the land looked as if it had come down with mange. Many huge patches had been sprayed from the air with herbicides to keep down "undesirable" hardwoods and to produce more spruce, which is easiest to use for paper; in the middle of summer the leaves of the dying trees were awash with the colors of autumn. In some places the Allagash Wilderness Waterway was instantly recognizable, for a line of trees a few hundred feet wide ran along each side of it; from a canoe in the river it appears that you are in wilderness, an illusion that would be shattered if you walked a quarter mile to pee and found yourself staring out across a plain nearly devoid of life. In recent years new legislation (written with the help of the forest-products industry) has limited the size of clearcuts. In some places loggers have actually begun to make less damaging but still very heavy partial cuts; in other spots the main result is that now strange geometric figures are cut from the forest, huge assemblages of clearcuts separated by narrow "wildlife corridors" that lead nowhere.

As we flew over the wasted woods, my companions kept shouting above the noise of the engines as we spotted new outrages. A whole series of new logging roads is clearly visible running right to the border of Baxter State Park, home of Mount Katahdin and the only sizable public holding in the state. We flew west for a few minutes: "That's the Ragmuff area," noted Michael Kellett, director of the environmental group RESTORE. "Thoreau wrote about it. It looks like it could be Kansas now—a few little clumps of trees and then vast fields." Engholm takes up passengers every week or so to let them see the damage firsthand. "Almost universally, they are just aghast when they see it. It's not any one cut in particular—it's that they just go on and on and on. There's no place in Maine where from a couple of thousand feet up you don't see a manipulated forest."

With the old trees gone, the loggers return ever more quickly for the young ones. You see log trucks in Maine with eighty or a hundred skinny trunks in one load, where once only a score would have fit.

The clearcutting of Maine's North Woods, according to Kellett, has proceeded faster, relative to their size, than the clearing of the Amazon. In some years 200,000 acres in the state are clearcut or high-graded, and thousands of miles of roads have been cut since the river drives ended in the early 1960s. (From the air we clocked log-truck drivers, some of whom are paid piecework rates rather than salaries, topping ninety miles per hour on the gravel roads, their rooster tails of dust visible twenty miles away.)

A few days after the flight, I visited Mitch Lansky, a North Woods resident who began to investigate the forest industry after being sprayed with pesticides from a modified World War II bomber while he was leaving for work at the local mill. He unrolled an enormous photo for me on the floor of his cabin. "I want to show you what northern Maine looks like from outer space," he says. "This is a satellite photo from 1990, and these white spots are six-mile-by-six-mile townships. Just in this one little corner are a hundred and thirty square miles of clearcuts." Lansky took me for a drive around his Wytopitlock home, where the clearcuts stretched for miles. They are growing back with poplar, which once comprised less than two percent of the forest. "One other species does really well," says Lansky. "Raspberries."

The overcutting is not confined to the North Woods, either. In the Southeast, along the Smokies and the Blue Ridge, clearcuts have sprouted in recent years as well, often on national forest land owned by the federal government. When Washington first acquired the land around the turn of the century, most of it was so wrecked by logging and poor farming that large areas simply had to be given a rest. "It was decimated from the top of the ridge to the creek bank," says Brent Connor, an attorney with Asheville's Southern Appalachia Biodiversity Project. "So for half a century the only management on Forest Service land was to sit back and let it recover. Fire suppression, that was it." But as nature rejuvenated the land, the Forest Service began to lease it off to loggers. Connor, an unreconstructed Confederate who enjoys dressing up in gray and reenacting the Civil War with other buffs (and whose Daddy preaches at his Faith Tabernacle, "where there's no law but love, no Lord but Christ, no book but the Bible"), found himself standing on a logging road in the Pisgah National Forest one day during hunting season, staring down a logging truck. "They had gone berserk, so I was starting to go berserk. I stood there one day with my bow and arrow and forced a logging truck to go around me." His anger has since been channeled into more serious pestering: filing suits to prevent cutting on federal tracts across the Southeast. "People ask me, 'Don't you think the Lord can take care of this?'" he says. "I tell them, 'Sure—it's the Forest Service that's the trouble.'"

Many Americans don't know that the national forests are open to loggers—a mistake the Forest Service does its best to encourage with wooden signs closely resembling those found at the entrance to national parks and with careful planning to ensure that the clearcuts allowed by the feds are screened from passing motorists by a strip of trees. But on both public and private land across the Southeast, clearcutting—the relentless removal of almost every tree in a given area, a technique made especially easy with new machinery that allows one man sitting in the cab of a giant machine to cut and carry many trees at a time—is just another typical order of business. The technique is more damaging than older forms of forestry—when they used horses, loggers left behind the old and rotten trees, which soon fell and decayed into nursery beds for new trees, as well as the immature saplings, which provided some shade. Now, from a barren clearcut, the foresters use all the tools in their arsenal to "manage" for particular outcomes—a stand of same-size yellow poplar, for instance, which might reach "financial maturity" in forty years and then be cut again.

The paper companies and timber barons have mounted a large-scale public-relations campaign to persuade people not to trust the feeling in their gut that comes from looking at the ugly face of industrial forestry. "Trees are renewable resources" was the industry mantra for years, finally eroded by the growing realization that it wasn't simply the number of trunks that mattered, but the quality of the forest. More recently, trying to co-opt the alarm over biodiversity, the industry argued that clearcuts create more "edge"—good for certain species of wildlife, such as white-tailed deer. But it is abundantly clear that the forests the huge companies are creating resemble a real Maine woods or North Carolina forest about as closely as extruded seafood product resembles lobster. Thoreau wrote of the Maine woods that "the surface is everywhere spongy and saturated with moisture. I noticed that the plants which cover the forest floor there are commonly confined to swamps with us." Now, with sunlight streaming into the clearcuts, the forest can dry.

A recent study of national forests in western North Carolina found that catches of salamanders were five times as high in mature stands as in forests clearcut less than ten years ago. Because they need to keep their skin wet to breathe, salamanders generally keep to moist microhabitats. A clearcut, which leaves an unshaded field, dehydrates the forest floor, reduces leaf litter, and increases soil temperature. All in all, says James Petranka of the University of North Carolina, the clearcutting is killing 14 million salamanders annually. And when it comes back, the clearcut is often no longer a forest—it's an "even-aged" stand, maybe composed almost entirely of a single species. "The 'working forest,' industry's current euphemism, is classic *Nineteen Eighty-four* doublespeak," says Kellett. "It sounds industrious, it sounds healthy, but it's a disaster. It's a factory."

One of the most destructive aspects of industrial forestry is the network of roads it demands. The river drives were far from ecologically benign, scouring the banks year after year; but the Maine environmentalists who worked to outlaw them in the 1960s did not anticipate the speed with which the logging companies would build roads through the area: since 1970 about twelve thousand miles of road have been built, so that no spot in the North Woods is more than two miles from a road. The publicly owned national forests, especially in the Southeast, are no better—some contain as many as eight miles of road for every square mile of forest, and Forest Service plans call for nearly tripling the number of roads in the next four decades. "Ninety percent of the southern Appalachians is within half a mile of a road passable by a four-wheel-drive vehicle," says forest researcher Dan Boone, a distant relation of the man who found his way west on foot.

Narrow, lightly traveled backcountry roads may not seem like a great threat to the natural world they bisect, but Reed Noss—the editor of the journal *Conservation Biology* who has written extensively on the subject—says their impact begins with the noise caused by construction and escalates from there. Exotic species invade along roads, from the *Melaleuca* trees now spreading across the Everglades to "opportunistic wildlife" like cowbirds and starlings that steal the nests of meeker species or dine on their eggs. Chipmunks, squirrels, and mice often won't cross roads even fifty feet wide for fear of ending up in some hawk's gullet; each new road circumscribes their universe. Other animals are attracted to roads: snakes to bask in the heat, birds to eat gravel that helps them digest seeds, deer to browse on the luxurious roadside vegetation, songbirds to dustbathe on dirt roads. By conservative estimate, a million animals are killed by cars on roads each day in the United States, many on small back roads. In Florida, where road mileage has increased 4.6 miles per day for the last fifty years, 65 percent of Florida panther deaths are roadkill; cars are even the main cause of mortality for the Florida scrub jay.

As roads have spread across the backcountry, they have changed human behavior, too. Hunting transformed itself in this century from the market-driven business that claimed entire species like the passenger pigeon into a sport that recaptured at least some of the ancient link between predator and prey. I have neighbors who depend on the deer they take in the fall to fill their freezers all winter, and they depend at least as much on the communion with the woods that good hunting produces. The spread of roads is shifting the sport once more, however—this time in the direction of a deadly, motorized laziness that gives all advantage to the guy with the gun. In Maine the timber companies lease bearbaiting sites to guides, who drive their clients there. At the sites, right along roads, bait— often raw french fries from the nearby Aroostook County processing plants—is set out on the ground, and the hunter installed in a tree-stand a few feet away. When a bear wanders in to investigate, he turns into a trophy. A new tribe, the "heater hunters," rarely leave their cars or pickups, unless it's to climb aboard a four-wheeler; if they have a moose permit, they'll cruise the logging roads until a moose appears along the shoulder. "Some people ride the roads for grouse," a Maine hunter told *Yankee* magazine in 1992. "They drive three thousand miles a week in October. I call it 'shoulder-sniping.' Open a window and shoot, or ride in an open-topped vehicle like a Jeep and just stand up and blast away."

★   ★   ★

Big-time logging does bring one blessing, however. For all the traumas industrial forestry continues to inflict on the land, you can fly for hours over northern Maine, or drive for days in the national forests farther south, and see no houses. Logging roads, clearcuts, gravel pits, and areas decimated by herbicides, but no subdivisions, shopping malls, and vacation resorts—the other great peril to this region—that threaten to fragment and degrade habitat even more effectively than did the farmer's fields plowed two centuries ago.

"We have two armies of occupation in this state," says poet and environmental organizer Gary Lawless, a native of Maine. "There are the paper companies in the north, and along the coast the people who move here for a better life and change it in a different way. They're clearcutting it, too, only very small pieces. And once they're here, they don't want certain things. They don't want fishing boat motors at four in the morning. They don't want bait in the sun on a hot day. They don't want chickens walking across the road." In far-northern New Hampshire, says newspaper editor John Harrigan, "every year there are more of those all-night lights where there used to be darkness. Little by little it's happening everywhere. Where I used to sit and look at a dark ridge, every night another all-night light seems to wink on. People from away come here, and they think darkness is the enemy—bears or bogeymen or something." People bring pavement, too, points out Harrigan; troublesome as a dirt road or a clearcut can be, "once you've paved it, you've changed it forever."

Perhaps the paradigm of such development can be found forty miles from the middle of Manhattan, in Sterling Forest, woods that straddle New York and New Jersey. A century ago it was denuded, destroyed by more than a hundred years of firing iron smelters. (The great chain that the Continental Army stretched across the Hudson to block British ship traffic during the Revolution was forged in Sterling Forest.) But like so much of the East, it slowly grew back. Now it is a 17,500-acre patch of green full of rattlesnake and bear, a critical path for migrating birds. Only one problem, again typical of the recovering East: the nicer it gets, the more valuable it becomes. At the moment, the corporation that owns it wants to develop it into five planned towns: 13,000 units of housing, 8 million square feet of industrial and commercial space. The business plan quotes Wendell Berry on the need for environmental stewardship, and indeed the corporation is plotting carefully clustered homes with a lot of open space. But when the developers finish, the unbroken forest will be gone, replaced by a chain of suburbs that together will constitute one of the largest towns between New York and Albany.

Sue Sharko, who grew up in the area, and John Gebhards, who heads a coalition of environmentalists trying to persuade the state and federal governments to buy and preserve the land, took me hiking one afternoon on the Appalachian Trail, which runs within a few hundred feet of one of the planned communities. "This is literally less than an hour from Manhattan," says Sharko, pointing to a surging brook with worn hemlocks leaning out across it. "Not much less, maybe three minutes less, but still. . . ." Every time we reach a vantage point, Gebhards points to the next ridge and says, "That's going to be the new town of Tuxedo Estates" or "That's going to be one of the golf courses." (There are three courses planned for the site.) It was a magnificent spring day, and from the highest spots along the trail, though you're within a two-hour drive of one American in twelve, you see nothing but forest stretching off in the distance. The view was powerful testimony to the enormous vigor of the natural world, even on the edge of the megalopolis. But we're trained not to see it. Gebhards says the national environmental groups have endorsed his campaign, but it's been hard to convince them to devote any of their lobbyists' time to winning the congressional battle for funds to save the tract, possibly because "no one really believes there could be something like this near the city," he says. Leon Billings, a lobbyist for the developers, is more explicit. His childhood in Montana filled him with "an absolute admiration for the wilderness," he tells a newspaper reporter. But to speak of Sterling Forest in the same breath was "ludicrous," because it isn't virgin land. "We're not talking Glacier National Park here," he says. "This isn't even farmland in Virginia. This is an area that was at one time industrialized." By that reckoning, there's hardly an inch of the East that should be off limits.

And, in fact, some of the areas that have been most recently degraded by logging are under the greatest threat of development. One of the biggest fears of eastern environmentalists is that the twin plagues of industrial forestry and overdevelopment will join at the waist: that in New England, for instance, the forest-products industry—which for all the damage it has caused has at least kept the vast

woodlands it manages free of houses and pavement, and thus theo-
retically restorable—might decide to start selling off the land it has
degraded. A single deal, one that speaks eloquently of the emerging
global economy, touched off huge worries about a decade ago. In the
early Reagan years, a British financier named Sir James Goldsmith
took over the Diamond Corporation, a forest-products company
that owned about a million acres in New England and New York.
He quickly sold off most of the divisions of the company, thereby
recouping nearly all the $660 million he had spent on the company
and leaving him with all the land, mostly undeveloped forest. This
he peddled to a French conglomerate, which promptly put much of
it on the market for sale to the highest bidder. The region's economy was booming, and the demand for second homes climbing—
a forty-acre lot on Moosehead Lake in Maine, which sold for
$50,000 in 1986, went for $250,000 in 1988. It was easy to imagine
the Loon-Cry Estates and Trillium Manors spreading across the
New England landscape as quickly as the clearcuts; the economic
term is "highest and best use" of the land. Because developers really
want river or lake frontage, journalist Ted Williams pointed out in
Audubon magazine, "highest and best use translates to suburbaniza-
tion of remote watersheds," of the very places most essential to this
rebirth of wildness.

*   *   *

There's a shorter and more universal way to say what I've been trying
to say: the resurgent health of the place where I live is threatened by
wealth. Not so much the wealth of its residents, who, relative to other
Americans, are poor—are Appalachian. But wealth in general, the

universal cult of economic expansion. Forests, for instance, fall to the incredible desire for paper and timber; shorelines are overbuilt by the desire for second homes.

Some of the problems are relatively easy to solve, at least in theory: with new wilderness areas, new logging regulations, and new zoning, we could slowly bring them to heel. But there is an even larger sense in which the relentless growth in human appetites erodes the fabric of this place: in the most fundamental and practical ways, the problems of the maple and the moose can only be tackled by taking on the culture of materialism and the accompanying erosion of community.

Consider a study conducted some years ago by Charles Hall, a Syracuse professor. He calculated that every American dollar or its equivalent spent anywhere on earth triggered a series of events that, on average, consumed half a liter of petroleum. Spend twenty dollars on a book and—between the logging and the pulping and the printing and the shipping and the advertising—you've used up a couple of gallons of oil. Burn a gallon of oil and you release about five pounds of carbon into the atmosphere. So this tome represents maybe a ten-pound cloud of CO_2—the most important of the greenhouse gases, the most important human pollutant yet devised. Spend two hundred dollars on a suit and emit a few hundred pounds of carbon dioxide. The figures are not exact, obviously, but they make the point: money is a scrip redeemed in, among other things, units of pollution. With every normal action in a consumer society, we nudge the thermometer a little higher. Wealth—and hence consumption—degrades the planet, degrades it as surely as stark poverty, which is environmentally damaging for other reasons.

It is true that more money can clean up certain problems.

Expensive filters have helped cut California's smog and clean the Great Lakes. But there are no filters for the most disastrous types of pollution; there is nothing you can put on your car engine or your smokestack to reduce the amount of carbon dioxide produced for each gallon of gas or ton of coal burned. You can only drive less and use less—which we have steadfastly refused to do. If there are underdeveloped nations on this planet, there are also overdeveloped ones; and most of the people reading this book live in them. Simply by living according to the customs of such places, each of us powers the planet's decline. We don't need to own strip mines or chop down ancient forests—our daily life is sufficient.

Or forget the sermon, and let's put it this way: computer projections of climate change indicate that by the end of the next century, hemlock trees—which shade the streams in the place where I live, cooling the water for the trout—may not survive south of the Canadian border. Our ways of life daily edge us closer to full-scale ecological disintegration: the cascading loss of species, the violent swings in weather, all the other unpredictable devastations of an overheated world.

And so, to think clearly about my own place requires coming to terms with these ways of life. When I wrote *The End of Nature*, my prescription was vaguer than my diagnosis. We must learn to live more humbly, I argued, for improved technology would be insufficient to offset the crisis. I believe more than ever that this is the case. But what does "humbly" mean? Are there ways to live that both satisfy human desires and pay attention to the limits placed on us by the planet?

Some people try to answer that question through engineering, and their efforts are clearly part of the solution. With windmills and solar cars and so on, perhaps we can someday reach the point where spending a dollar only demands a quarter liter of oil. But in the meantime, of course, we seem bent on doubling, trebling, quadrupling the size of our economies, and hence wiping out whatever advantage we gain through efficiency. Gregg Easterbrook, one of the most convinced environmental optimists of the moment, wrote in 1994 that energy consumption per unit of GNP had fallen 1 percent a year in the United States since 1973. Which is nice; but since the GNP was rising at nearly 3 percent a year, the amount of fuel we used—the amount of carbon we spewed into the atmosphere—continued to rise. In the 1980s, despite a tremendous push by power companies for efficiency, American consumers increased their per capita electricity consumption 11 percent. Utilities offered rebates for installing compact fluorescent bulbs, and indeed between 1986 and 1991 the typical household added one such light. But the typical household also added more than seven incandescent lamps, going from twenty-eight to thiry-seven lights per house. And it is not just us, of course. China now adds a southern California's worth of generating capacity to its electric grid *each year*. Its coal reserves are deep enough to double the atmospheric concentration of carbon dioxide by themselves.

From an economic point of view, that's good news. We're producing more, trading more—that's how it's supposed to work. If you assembled all the world's politicos in one room—capitalists and socialists, Democrats and Republicans, Tories and populists, bureaucrats and ultranationalists—the one goal they could all happily endorse would be economic growth. In the memorable phrasing of candidate Clinton, "It's the economy, stupid." And yet through an environmental prism, such growth is disastrous. It means we grow larger each year, not smaller.

So the engineers, important as they are, won't save us. And anyway, I'm not an engineer; I'm a reporter. My response to this dilemma was to look out around the world for other places that seem to be working on less. Not for places where nature was necessarily healthy or particularly important, but for places that managed to produce decent human lives with less money, less energy, less wood. Less stuff. For places where people, in their wants and needs, were smaller. If there were such places, I wanted to see what lessons they might offer my home place, and all the other home places on the planet.

There are enormous obstacles to tracking down, even to imagining, such different kinds of happiness. The current flow of information around the world, for instance, hobbles our fancy. Where once we sent missionaries and soldiers to far-flung spots, we now send television images. Would it surprise you to learn that one billion people—one human in five—see the TV program *Baywatch* each week? That's more than take communion each week or bow toward Mecca; and, of course, it inspires others to worship the gods of our consumer pantheon. But the simple act of supplying all the images does at least as much damage here at home. We send out so much information that we receive very little ourselves; we get no sustained looks at other ways of life. It's as if we had a telephone that we could only talk into. And, at least from an environmental standpoint, *we* are the ones desperately in need of missionaries that could show us how to live closer to the ground. Little Sisters of the Rich.

The current spread of world trade, exemplified by the recent NAFTA and GATT deals, only exacerbates this problem. Increasingly, there *are* no other cultures and economies that might suggest different approaches to things; there is only one system, ours. Some places have working versions of our system, and other places find elves crushed by it; but nothing else is allowed: the International Monetary Fund and the World Bank have demanded that one poor country after another "structurally adjust" until its economy mirrors ours. In the end, argues Rensselaer economist Sabine O'Hara, we have endangered "socio-diversity" nearly as completely as biodiversity. Once there were different ideas about time, places, limits, and responsibility to neighbors. And these differences were vast—the gulf between a cyclical and a linear concept of time, for instance, is far more profound than the gulf between communism and capitalism. But as we've spread our system everywhere, these contrasts have been stamped out, limiting the gene pool from which new economies and societies might someday evolve.

So I counted myself fortunate to find two places that seemed to me grand exceptions to the general rule. Curitiba, a relatively poor city in the south of Brazil, has solved urban problems we find intractable even in the rich West. And the Indian state of Kerala, which is impoverished by any measure, proves that a high quality of life does not demand high levels of consumption. Their relative poverty is not incidental; it is precisely what makes them valuable as models.

Their lessons are mainly about learning to do with less, or at least with different—with buses instead of cars, with community instead of splendid suburban independence, with preventive health care instead of high-tech medicine, with creativity instead of big budgets, with sharing instead of individual accumulation. Their lessons are about expectations reduced—or at least very different—from the ones we currently take for granted. I found hope in these places, but no miracle cures, no Twinkie diets. The treatment they suggest has side effects. There are no fifty *simple* ways to save the planet; there are only a few difficult ways to learn to live within its bounds. And

they are most difficult for those of us so long accustomed to living outside its bounds.

In some ways, then, the diary of my journey is a primer for retreat, for climbing down from the untenable heights on which we find ourselves. For imagining new ways that might sustain natural recoveries—like the one I see around me in the East—and spread them to other corners of the globe. I understand all the practical objections to dramatic change; indeed, I feel them strongly in my own life. All the more important, then, to find real spots, look at them closely, and say, "This may be difficult but it's not, strictly speaking, *inconceivable*."

This book offers no utopias; indeed, as the word is commonly understood, we have been living in a utopia all our lives, a place as sumptuously appointed and as divorced from physical labor as any in history. What I have been seeking instead are models of some post-utopia, places that resemble neither our pleasant daydream of a society nor the various nightmares so obvious in the world around us. Some places that make hope real, as real as it is here next to the beaver dam.

Chapter 2
CURITIBA

The first time I went there, I had never heard of Curitiba. I had no idea that its bus system was the best on earth, that it had largely solved the problem of streetchildren that plagues the rest of South America, or that a municipal shepherd and his flock of thirty sheep trimmed the grass in its vast parks. It was just a midsize Brazilian city where an airline schedule forced me to spend the night midway through a long South American reporting trip. I reached my hotel, took a nap, and then went out in the early evening for a walk—warily, because I had just come from crime-soaked Rio. But the street in front of the hotel was cobbled, closed to cars, and strung with lights. It opened onto another such street, which in turn opened into a broad and leafy plaza, with more shop-lined streets stretching off in all directions. Though the night was frosty—Brazil stretches well south of the tropics, and Curitiba is in the mountains—people strolled and shopped, butcher to baker to bookstore. There were almost no cars, but at one of the squares a steady line of buses rolled off, full, every few seconds. I walked for an hour, and then another;

I felt my shoulders, hunched from the tension of Rio (and probably New York as well) straightening. Though I flew out the next day as scheduled, I never forgot the city.

From time to time over the next few years, I would see Curitiba mentioned in planning magazines or come across a short newspaper account of it winning various awards from the United Nations. Its success seemed demographically unlikely. For one thing, it's relatively poor—average per capita income is about twenty-five hundred dollars. Worse, a flood of displaced peasants has tripled its population to a million and a half in the last twenty-five years. It should resemble a small-scale version of urban nightmares like São Paulo or Mexico City. But I knew, from my evening's stroll, it wasn't like that, and I wondered why.

It was more than idle curiosity. The longer I thought about my home place, the more I knew that its natural recovery was mostly a matter of luck and timing—that it could easily deteriorate again because people had not changed the economic habits or attitudes of mind that laid it waste in the first place. We still cherish notions of extreme individualism; if anything, our sense of community weakens more each year. Our politics is ever more firmly in the hands of those who exalt the private, those who write off whole swaths of people and places.

Although I no longer live an urban life, I knew that the key to many of these mysteries involved cities—and not simply because of their potential for environmental efficiency. More because they had long been the places where we worked out our most important accommodations. Where we built our most important links, however tenuously, between different kinds of people. Where sheer crowdedness made compromise essential. The erosion of the sense of community in the cities I knew—most especially New York, but in fact any place ringed with suburbs—seems to me to have signaled the erosion of *politics* as something useful, to have turned it from a source of togetherness and common feeling into a reflection of apartness and self-interest.

If any of my hopes for the small and lonely places I love best are ever to bear fruit, that cynical divisiveness has to be reversed. Maybe an effort to convince myself that such a decay in public life was not inevitable was why I went back to Curitiba to spend some real time, to see if its charms extend beyond the lovely downtown. For a month my wife and baby and I lived in a small apartment near the city center. Morning after morning I interviewed cops, merchants, urban foresters, civil engineers, novelists, planners; in the afternoons we pushed the stroller around the town, learning its rhythms and habits.

And we decided, with great delight, that Curitiba is among the world's great cities.

Not for its physical location: there are no beaches, no broad bridge-spanned rivers. Not in terms of culture or glamour: it's a fairly provincial place. But measured for "livability"—a weak coinage expressing some optimum mix of pleasures provided and drawbacks avoided—I have never been any place like it. In a recent survey 60 percent of New Yorkers wanted to leave their rich and cosmopolitan city; 99 percent of Curitibans told pollsters that they were happy with their town; and 70 percent of Paulistas, residents of the mobbed megalopolis to the north, said they thought life would be better in Curitiba. It has slums: some of the same shantytown *favelas* that dominate most Third World cities have sprouted on the edge of town as the population has rocketed. But even they are different, hopeful in palpable ways. They are clean, for instance—under a city

~~C\+\~~ program a slumdweller who collects a sack of garbage gets a sack of food from the city in return.

And Curitiba is the classic example of decent lives helping produce a decent environment. One statistic should underline the importance of this place to the world. Because of its fine transit system, and because its inhabitants are attracted toward the city center instead of repelled out to a sprawl of suburbs, Curitibans use 25 percent less fuel per capita than other Brazilians, even though they are actually more likely to own cars. Twenty five percent is a large enough number to matter; in the United States we are battling, unsuccessfully, merely to hold our much-higher fossil fuel use steady. And this 25 percent came before anyone redesigned cars or changed energy prices or did any of the other things only a federal government or an international treaty can do. It came not from preaching at folks about waste or ranting about global warming. It came from designing a city that actually meets people's desires, a city that is as much an example for the sprawling, decaying cities of the First World as for the crowded, booming cities of the Third World. A place that, at the very least, undercuts the despair that dominates every discussion of the world's cities, where half of human souls now reside.

It is a place, most of all, that helps redeem the idea of politics. If there's one lesson that Ronald Reagan and now Newt Gingrich have successfully hammered home to Americans, it's that "public"—education or transit or broadcasting or health care—is necessarily shabby and cumbersome, while "private" is shiny and efficient. Until that notion (which all too often reflects the present truth) changes, nothing will alter the basic momentum of our predicament. If Curitiba seems at first far removed from the forests and villages and suburbs of the rural East, it came to seem an absolutely essential first stop on my journey.

★   ★   ★

The Portuguese arrived on the Planalto, the first plateau above the Atlantic, in the middle of the seventeenth century. They were looking for gold, which was gone by 1660; a few stayed on to found a backwater town, Curitiba, which was known as the "sleeping city," a good stopover on the route to São Paulo. But the tea farms of Paraná state drew a steady stream of European immigrants—especially Italians, Poles, and Germans—many of whom eventually settled in Curitiba, the state's capital. By 1940 there were 125,000 residents. By 1950 the number had jumped to 180,000, and by 1960 doubled to 361,000— the explosive, confident growth that marked the entire country was underway in Curitiba as well. And with many of the same effects: traffic downtown started to snarl, and the air was growing thick with exhaust. It was clear that the time had come to plan; and as in almost every other city, planning meant planning for automobiles.

Curitiba's official scheme called for widening the main streets of the city to add more lanes, which would have meant knocking down the turn-of-the-century buildings that lined the downtown, and for building an overpass that would link two of the city's main squares by going over the top of Rua Quinze de Novembro, the main shopping street. Any American living in a city that has undergone urban renewal or been cut off from its waterfront by a belt of highway would recognize the plan in an instant; in one form or another, it's how urban areas around the globe have been reconfigured for the auto age.

But in Curitiba, resistance to the plan was unexpectedly fierce. Opposition was centered in the architecture and planning departments of the local branch of the federal university, and the loudest voice belonged to Jaime Lerner.

Jaime Lerner is a chubby man with a large, friendly, and open face. He looks like Norm, the guy at the end of bar in *Cheers*. He also looks silly stuffed into a suit; so even though he's been mayor of Curitiba on and off for the last two decades, he normally wears a blue polo shirt. He has an abiding interest in almost everything. His press secretary says that quite often, answering a question on television, Lerner "starts in about this city here that he's just visited, and this movie he was thinking about, and this book he just read. And I tell him, 'No, No, No—you need shock asterisks,'" the local translation of sound bite.

In the late 1960s, however, he was just a young planner and architect who had grown up in the city, working in his Polish father's dry goods store. And he organized the drive against the overpass, out of what might almost be called nostalgia. "They were trying to throw away the story of the city," he recalls; they were trying to emulate, on a much smaller scale, the tabula rasa "miracle" of Brasília—the capital city that was still being completed in the country's interior— perhaps the grandest stab at designing a city from the ground up in the world's history. Brasília was the buzz of architects and planners everywhere, and the country's greatest claim to modernity. Its site was chosen from aerial photographs of various scrublands and turned over to Oscar Niemeyer, the foremost Brazilian disciple of Le Corbusier; as Alex Shoumatoff, in his history of the city, writes: "Most of the young intellectuals in Latin America at that time were eager to break with the past and take a long leap forward." Their plan was for a rational grid of buildings precisely the same size, with a giant "Sector of Diversion" in the center. Functions were strictly separated—work in one area, shop in another, play in a third—and the regions were linked mainly by road. It was a "speedway city," to be built entirely without intersections; anyone walking between the monumental buildings would have to use overpasses. Construction drowned the richest forest on the central plateau, and the glass buildings baked like ovens in the sun—it is a city inconceivable without the air conditioner and the car. But never mind. Yuri Gagarin visited. "I feel as if I have just disembarked on another planet, not earth," he said, meaning it as a compliment. Malraux, speaking for European modernity, told a crowd that "a murmur of glory accompanies the pounding of the anvils that salute your audacity, your faith, and the destiny of Brazil, as the Capital of Hope surges on." Frank Capra thought it was the eighth wonder of the world.

With all that exaltation in the air, it was a good thing that Jaime Lerner had visited Paris as a young student and especially that he had grown up loving the mix of people in Curitiba. Because Lerner, through a chain of political flukes, found himself the mayor of Curitiba at the age of thirty-three. Brazil in the early 1970s was ruled by the military, and the local governor was not interested in appointing anyone who might turn out to be a political rival. He picked Lerner, who took the job despite his repugnance for the army. All of a sudden his friends and colleagues were pulling their plans out of the cupboards. All of a sudden they were going to get their chance to remake Curitiba—not for cars but for people. "I was born on the street of the central railroad station," says Lerner. "My father—he had a shop in this street, and we lived in the back of the business. I used, since six, to play in the street. Since my childhood I had everything from the street. Peasants, they came each day. We had big factories so I knew all kind of workers. We had the state assembly. The old streetcars. We had circus, newspapers. The whole life—hotels. So I could have an idea about the whole society. I was playing, and just watching. I never could forget this street, which was a street like other streets that everyone has in his life. But a street is the synthesis of the whole city, the whole society."

And so the story of Curitiba begins with its central street, Rua Quinze—the one that the old plan wanted to obliterate with an overpass. Lerner insisted instead that it should become a pedestrian mall, an emblem of his drive for a human-scale city. "I knew we'd have a big fight," he says. "I had no way to convince the storeowners a pedestrian mall would be good for them, because there was no other pedestrian mall in Brazil. No other in the world, really, except maybe Munich. But I knew if they had a chance to actually see it, everyone would love it." To prevent opposition, he planned carefully. "I told my staff, 'This is like a war.' My secretary of public works said the job would take two months. I got him down to one month. Maybe one week, he said, but that's final. I said, 'Let's start Friday night, and we have to finish by Monday morning.'" And they did jackhammering up the pavement, putting down cobblestones, erecting streetlights and kiosks, and putting in tens of thousands of flowers.

"It was a horrible risk—he could easily have been fired," says Oswaldo Alves, who helped with the work. But by midday Monday the same storeowners who had been threatening legal action were petitioning the mayor to extend the mall. The next weekend, when offended members of the local automobile club threatened to "reclaim" the street by driving their cars down it, Lerner didn't call out the police. Instead, he had city workers lay down strips of paper the length of the mall. When the auto club arrived, its members found dozens of children sitting in the former street painting pictures. The transformation of Curitiba had begun.

But this was not some romantic revolution, a cultural protest of the sort so common in the wake of the sixties and so evanescent. Even this small victory was possible only because Lerner and his architect friends had thought so carefully about the future of the city. They had, among other things, carefully replotted the city's traffic flow, not only to make the downtown function without cars on its main street, but also to direct growth throughout the city. Instead of buying up buildings and tearing them down to widen streets, planners stared at the maps long enough to see that the existing streets would do just fine—as long as they were considered in groups of three parallel avenues. Traffic on the first avenue would flow one way, into town. The middle street would be devoted to buses, driving in dedicated lanes so they could move more quickly. A block over you'd find motorists heading out of town. No highways in the city—three streets still scaled to human beings. And more important, once the planners had designated five of these "structural axes" leading out from the center of town like spokes in a wheel, they could begin to tinker with zoning. Along these main routes, high-density buildings were permitted—the apartments that would hold the commuters eager to ride the buses. Farther from the main roads, density decreases.

From the observation deck on the top of the city's television tower, you can see the results spread out below you: not a ring of high-rises choking the downtown, but orderly lines of big buildings shading off into neighborhoods along each of the axes; a city growing on linear lines that removed congestion from the center, and kept a mix of housing—and hence, of incomes—throughout the city. "Every city has its hidden designs—old roads, old streetcar ways," says Lerner. "You're not going to invent a new city. Instead, you're doing a strange archaeology, trying to enhance the old, hidden design. You can't go wrong if the city is growing along the trail of memory and of transport. Memory is the identity of the city, and transport is the future."

*   *   *

Transport in the case of Curitiba means buses. Though larger Brazilian cities were investing in subways and though "there were always people trying to sell them to us as the modern way," Lerner and his team decided the subways were too expensive—that they were stuck with buses. They also decided that buses needn't be stuck in traffic. They quickly designed the system of express lanes that sped travel to and from the downtown, and ridership began to take off. In 1974 the system carried 25,000 passengers a day; by 1993 the number was 1.5 million—or more than ride the buses in New York City each day. The route network looks like a model of the human brain. Orange feeder buses and green buses traveling in constant loops through the outer neighborhoods deliver passengers to terminals, where they catch red express buses heading downtown or out to the factories on the city's edge.

In an effort to increase speed even further, the red express buses were replaced in the late 1980s by silver "direct line" buses on the busiest streets. The buses move faster not because they have bigger motors but because they were designed by smarter people. Sitting at a bus stop one day, Lerner noticed that the biggest time drag on his fleet was how long it took passengers to climb the stairs and pay the fare. He sketched a plan for a glass "tube station," a bus shelter raised off the ground and with an attendant to collect fares. When the bus pulls in, its doors open like a subway's, and people walk right on (or, in the case of wheelchairs, roll right on). A year after the "speedybuses" went into service, the city did a survey: 28 percent of the passengers were new to the system, commuters who had parked their cars because of the new convenience. In 1993 Curitiba added another Lerner innovation—extra-long buses, hinged in two spots to snake around corners and able to accommodate three hundred passengers. Five doors open and close at each stop, and on busy routes at rush hour one of these behemoths arrives every minute or so; twenty thousand passengers an hour can move in one direction. There is a word for this kind of service: subway.

Amazingly, the city doesn't need to subsidize its bus service. The fleet is purchased and owned by private companies; the government assigns routes, sets fares, and pays each contractor by kilometer traveled. For about thirty cents, you can transfer as often as you want; and the whole network turns a profit. A few years ago, to help celebrate Earth Day, Curitiba lent New York several of its loading tubes and special buses. Brazilians installed the system in five days, and for a couple of months the buses plied a loop from the Battery to South Street Seaport and back. The *Daily News* reported "looks of bewilderment" at the "space age pod" donated by the Third World to the absolute epicenter of world finance, but by all accounts passengers loved the system. Still, it seems to have disappeared into some bureaucratic maw. The New York City bus system has seen ridership fall 42 percent in the last twenty years and is only now beginning to experiment with "innovations" like stopping every third block instead of every second one. The "realistic hope," according to a recent Transit Authority report, is that ridership will fall only 7 percent this decade. I understand why; I never rode the buses when I lived in New York. I could walk faster than a rush-hour bus in midtown, and the rest of the day they rarely came; the windows were so scratched that once you were on board you had to peer owl-eyed to see if your stop was approaching. But in Curitiba I rode every day, pushing my daughter's stroller onto the bus, finding my way more easily than in Manhattan despite my pidgin Portuguese. *The bus serves you*, and not the other way around; you feel in control of the city, not a victim of its tie-ups and bottlenecks and ancient every-day-repeated traffic jams.

★   ★   ★

The public relations man for the transit system, Norberto Staviski, was showing me a video made in the early 1980s about the evolution of the buses. At one point, the film's narrator explains that traffic is growing too dense for the buses along the busiest routes and that they will soon be replaced by an electric tramway. Staviski leaped up and stopped the tape—"we *did* consider a tramway," he said. "But it just turned out to be too expensive." Hence, the brainstorming that led to the tube stations and the triple-length buses, which carry four times as many passengers each day as Rio's subway system and cost one-half of one percent as much per kilometer.

Cheapness is one of the three cardinal dictates of Curitiban planning. Many of the city's buildings are "recycled." The planning headquarters is in an old furniture factory; the gunpowder depot became a furniture factory; a glue plant was turned into the children's center.

An old trolley stationed on the Rua Quinze has become a free baby-sitting center where shoppers can park their kids for a few hours.

The city's parks provide the best example of brilliance on the cheap. When Lerner took office for the first time in 1971, the only park in Curitiba was smack downtown—the Passeio Público, a cozy zoo and playground with a moat for paddleboats and a canopy of old and beautiful *ipé* trees, which blossom blue in the spring. "In that first term, we wanted to develop a lot of squares and plazas," recalls Alves. "We picked one plot, we built a lot of walls, and we planted a lot of trees. And then we realized this was very expensive."

At the same time, as luck would have it, most Brazilian cities were installing elaborate flood-control projects. Curitiba had federal money to "channelize" the five rivers flowing through town, putting them in concrete viaducts so that they wouldn't flood the city with every heavy summer rain and endanger the buildings starting to spring up in the floodplain. "The bankers wanted all the rivers enclosed," says Alves; instead, city hall took the same loan and spent it on land. At a number of sites throughout the city, engineers built small dams and backed up the rivers into lakes. Each of these became the center of a park; and if the rains were heavy, the lake might rise a foot or two—perhaps the jogging track would get a little soggy or the duck in the big new zoo would find itself swimming a few feet higher than usual. "Every river has a right to overflow," insists parks chief Nicolau Klupel, who became known as "Nicolago."

Mostly because of its flood-control scheme, in twenty years—*even as it tripled in population*—the city went from two square feet of green area per inhabitant to more than a hundred and fifty square feet per inhabitant. The official literature always points out, with understandable pride, that this figure is four times the World

Health Organization standard of twelve square meters. From every single window in Curitiba, I could see as much green as I could concrete. And green begets green; land values around the new parks have risen sharply, and with them tax revenues.

The entire city government runs on a $250 million budget, or about $156 per capita, compared with, say, $807 per person in Dallas or $1,279 per person in Detroit. The municipal obsession with parsimony would amaze anyone used to traveling in the developing world, where visitors are invariably taken to huge and ostentatious showplace buildings in an attempt to prove the modernity and power of the government—in an attempt to show that they're as good as anyone else. In Curitiba, by contrast, I spent a typically dusty day with two of the local public housing authority officials, who were busy setting up a program that allowed newly arrived peasants to build tiny houses of their own for the price of two packs of cigarettes a month. After we looked over dozens of these new homes, the officials took me by a grand edifice that I'd noticed on the horizon—it turned out to be a school, built by Brazil's *federal* government (a government that may lead the world in corruption and inefficiency). Perched above a *favela*, the school had a lovely basketball court, just like you might find in a prosperous suburban high school in the United States. But dust was an inch thick on the parquet floor, and none of the classrooms were in use, either—in part because there were no desks, chairs, or other furnishings. "Someone ate up the in-between money," says one of the housing guys. "When I think of what we could do if we had the cash that went into this place . . ."

Simple is brother to cheap, and it's another of the mantras Curitiba's builders chant regularly. "The cities of the future will not be scenarios from *Flash Gordon*, as some people imagine," says Lerner.

("Nor scenarios from *Blade Runner*, as others, tied to an overpessimistic view, may fear.") Instead of supermen, their heroes will likely be people like Joao "Janguinho" Jorge, who was sitting on a sprung desk chair in a cluttered room off the bus repair station on the outskirts of the city when I interviewed him. He began his transit career in 1967 as a fare collector; by the time that Lerner's fancy new express buses came along, he was a top driver, one of those selected to train on the new equipment that Volvo was producing. On a regular bus, it doesn't make much difference where you stop—the passengers will just walk a few steps to board. But with the tube stations, the bus has to be in just the right place, or the openings on the tube won't align with the bus doors. Volvo was planning on installing an elaborate optical computer system.

"I said, 'Let's try a stripe painted on the pavement,'" recalls Janguinho. "And they said it wouldn't work. But I said, 'Let me try it once, I'll *see* if it works.' And it did." It's the kind of solution that gets you noticed in Curitiba; everyone kept telling me I had to go interview Janguinho, who was promoted to driving instructor and is now working on the one defect of superlong double-hinged buses: "If there's an accident ahead of you and you have to back up to get around it, it's kind of like driving a serpent."

"It's very hard to understand simplicity," says Lerner. "Simplicity needs a kind of commitment. You have to be sure of yourself. If you're not, you'll listen to the complexity-sellers, and the city is not as complex as they would like you to believe."

New York provides an apt illustration. Six years ago the city's Legal Action Center for the Homeless issued a report on public toilets in the city. Volunteers checked bathrooms in subways and parks and found that almost none were open; in those that were, "urine,

feces, newspaper, and stagnant water covered the floors, sinks, uri-
nals, and toilets." They also collected affidavits from homeless men
and women: "I have a diuretic condition, so I have to move my bow-
els every two hours," one reported. "If I try to hold it in, I get terrible
cramps. These cramps feel like a hot poker in my gut. . . . At least
once a month or so I can't find any place at all to go before it's too
late. Usually there are people around. What I do then is soil myself."
The Legal Action Center even came up with a solution, sidewalk
stalls of a sort already in use in Europe. They would have cost the
city nothing—the company puts them up in return for the advertising space. A small trial went quite well. But then the process ground
to a halt. For a year disability advocates demanded that *every* toilet
accommodate the handicapped; their demand was granted. Then
the whole proposal disappeared into some bureaucratic purgatory.
At the moment, a two-year study is underway to determine how
much advertising should be allowed on the stalls. Complexity has
overwhelmed common sense, and so more people—tired of pools
of urine—will move their families to Scarsdale. It would not have
happened that way in Curitiba.

Along with frugality and simplicity, Curitiba stresses speed.
When Lerner ripped up the main street and reassembled it as
a pedestrian mall over a single weekend, he set a precedent his
administrations have followed ever since. "Public work is always
linked to easygoing work in people's minds," he says. "With speed
comes credibility." The city's showcase Opera House, a steel-and-
glass birdcage set dramatically in an abandoned stone quarry next
to a spectacularly lit waterfall, was built in a month; one big park
was carved out in twenty days because officials feared it was about
to be invaded by slums.

"Jaime has a saying," explains his director of job training, Ester Proveller. "Don't wait until all your pumpkins are in the truck to start your journey to market. They'll accumulate along the way." (For the same reason, she adds, many of the city's most important officials are women. "He says if women get two good cards, they'll start to play. Men sit and wait for a whole hand. We're not as afraid of failure—in that way we're more brave.")

Christine Braga helped implement the city's voluntary, and highly successful, recycling program within a matter of months after it was first suggested. "It was like during a war," she says fondly. "We didn't have any time to make researches then. We had to establish it and implement. It's been going since 1989, and we only started to finally collect the data last year."

Lerner "pushes very much," adds Proveller, who is also his sister-in-law. "If you say, 'I'll need three months for this part, and three months for this part, and three months for this,' he says, 'Okay, you have three months. Total.' We used to say he consulted with oracles to set the dates, but to tell you the truth, everything comes out finished."

Part of the emphasis on speed stems from Brazil's system of term limits. Mayors can serve only one term and then have to step aside for four years—Lerner has been hop-scotching in and out of office since the early 1970s. In the words of a former president, Juscelino Kubitschek, "it is an ancient tradition in Brazil that no administration has ever brought to a successful conclusion any work initiated by its antecedent." But Lerner's commitment to quickness is more than tactical; he has an ideology of speed as well. Only local governments can move nimbly, he insists, and it's one of the reasons he thinks cities will be more important than nations in solving environmental problems. "More and more we have resentments against central governments," he says. "More and more we're used to quick answers. Technology has given this to us. Credit cards give us goods quickly, the fax machine gives us the message quickly—the only thing left in our Stone Age is the central governments."

★ ★ ★

Everywhere I went in official Curitiba, I met architects—architects designing bus systems, sewer networks, housing programs. Occasionally I'd come across a civil engineer, but almost everyone would sooner or later take out a piece of paper and start drawing a diagram. "I like to work with journalists, too," says Lerner, when I point this out to him. "You know why? Because journalists have to finish their work every day." When he can, he avoids working with experts. "Transport is so important, you can't leave it to experts," he told me one day. "They will solve the problem of transportation, but they won't link it to the problem of the city. When you realize how many cities were killed by traffic engineers, well, we should beat them with slippers, we really should." Similarly, he says, "we have a lot of mayors who are very good at budgets. But it isn't ultimately a problem of budgets." Or of laws or sociology, to name the two other lenses American politicians tend to look through.

What's useful about architects, I decided after a month in Curitiba, is that they're used to solving problems. They don't come back to you and say, "There's no way to put a house on that lot." They come back with ideas. They see the world visually, physically; they see not despair and difficulty, but simply constraints around which to work. "In many cities a lot of people are specialists in proving it's impossible to do things," says Lerner. "I try to work with professionals who think it's possible." His method is the method of architectural schools everywhere: "We use the charette, always the charette," he says, referring to the exercises in which students are given a challenge and then a few hours to sketch out some solutions.

Out of these skull sessions come innovations large and small. Curitiba now has a "twenty-four-hour street," a block-long covered arcade near the city center with shops and restaurants that never close. It grew out of Lerner's realization that "million-dollar structures remain vacant in off-peak hours, while the pressure for space is a major factor in urban tension." And the creativity is contagious. Planners from other cities spent a few days in the city last year for an exercise. For a while they stayed stiff and formal, more interested in speechifying than in sketching. Eventually, though, they met the mayor, who told them his secret of creativity: "You have to have fun. All my work, all my life, we have fun. We're laughing all the time. We're working on things that make us happy." Before they went home, one team of visitors designed a "toy factory," a big canvas tent that can move from one poor neighborhood to another, where children could be taught to make toys from recycled trash. The favorite toy? A plastic mineral water bottle laid on its side and decorated to look like a tube station for the speedybus.

The fact that the toy factory was quickly set up and still travels about the city helps explain another of the reasons Lerner has such dedicated colleagues. There are bright designers and architects the world over, but most of them labor in university departments; they have to scratch for years to get their best projects built. It's true that a senior architect in Curitiba's planning department may make three or four hundred dollars a month, which doesn't go much further than three or four hundred dollars in America. "Sometimes we are down because of the money," says city planner Liana Vallicelli. "But then along comes some beautiful project. It's possible to see these things actually get done."

And what makes for high morale, says Lerner, makes for effective government as well. "You have to begin the game. You don't have to have all the answers before you start—you can't be such smart guys. To start is important."

Lerner lives in a small house, which he designed for himself when he was still an architecture student. "When I was having it built, we came to the fireplace, which was very hard to build. And I had an old guy, who was a master bricklayer, working on it. He said to me, 'This is hard. But I'll make it. There are two types of master bricklayers: a master to make it happen, or a master to tell you it can't be done. I'm one of the ones who make it happen.' Many years later, when I was mayor, I went down to see the Third Age members off on their trip. [Curitiba, needless to say, has a massive municipal senior citizens program.] There were thousands of people there—a kilometer-long convoy of buses. But I saw that old bricklayer, and I said to him, I remember you. You don't have any idea how important you were to my life.'"

Lerner—and Curitiba—seems to have shed ideology in the name of constructive pragmatism. Building things to human scale may be an ideology of sorts, but it's outside of the political dialogue. In the argument between private and public that occupies center stage in America, for instance, Curitiba persists in choosing from column A and column B, entirely according to success. It gave buses priority over cars, which sounds vaguely liberal, but it let private companies run the buses when the speedybus system was installed, the city spent $4.5 million putting up tube stations, and the private companies spent $45 million buying buses. On the other hand, it told the bus companies what fare they could charge.

Life without political fetishes seems necessary to the freewheeling creativity of the place. Consider trees, for instance. The city began from the position that it liked them, liked them a lot. It planted trees all over town: one of Lerner's first slogans was, "We provide the shade, you provide the water." But the government did not stop there, with a "normal" public role. It also decreed strict limits on people's ability to cut down their own trees on their own land. I spent an instructive day with Edison Reva and Damaris Da Silva Seraphim, two of Curitiba's urban foresters. Their office was piled high with folders from recent cases: a man who'd been fined 136,500 cruzeiros ($800) for cutting fifteen trees without a license, a man granted permission to take down a diseased maple. "It's impossible to cut a tree without a license," says Damaris. "You ask for the license, and we go analyze the situation. There has to be a cause—the risk of damage, disease, it's in the way of construction. Not just because you're tired of looking at it." If you do cut a tree, you have to plant two more to take its place. Oh, and don't cut a flowering *ipé* or an *auracaria*, the native Paraná pine, or the fine is doubled. Edison put on his official vest and took out his ticket pad, and we set off on the day's rounds, checking out some of the new complaints phoned in overnight on the tree hotline and following up on old offenders to make sure trees had been replanted. We stopped at one small plot where a wealthy man had illegally cut down perhaps a half-acre to use as a vegetable garden. It was slowly reverting to woods, but Edison saw several evergreens that had died; he made a note to call the man and have him plant some more.

It sounds vaguely authoritarian, and yet from any high spot in town you see puffs of trees everywhere you look. Many streets are totally canopied, tunnels of green. And as the trees have grown, so has their popularity. We stopped to look at some sidewalk trees—*Coorticaeria*, gorgeous trees but the wrong ones to have planted along the street, since they have begun to drop branches on the power lines, and their roots are cracking the pavement. "But we can't just take them down," Edison says. "People would go crazy." In a solution that seemed to me very Curitiban, they had planted other trees all up and down the street. In seven or eight years they would be high enough to really shade the sidewalk, and only then would the chainsaw crew be sent out for the problem trees.

In a world of cities, states, and nations increasingly whipsawed by the demands of business, perhaps the best example of the value of Curitiba's independence is its Industrial City. When Lerner took over as mayor for the first time, he realized that the city needed industry: its traditional role as a governmental and financial center couldn't support the population boom that was clearly coming, and also couldn't underwrite the aggressive programs he had in mind. He could have simply offered huge tax breaks to anyone who promised jobs. Instead, acting quickly before speculators could run up the price, the city used eminent domain to purchase about forty square kilometers of land seven miles from downtown—seven miles *downwind* of downtown. The government put in streets and services, housing and schools, and linked the area solidly to the bus system, building a special "worker's line" that ran to the biggest poor neighborhood. It also enacted a series of regulations—stiff laws on air and water pollution and on the conservation of green space. (Only six square miles are actually available for building factories, and almost as large an area has remained planted in trees.) "What we've found is that regulation attracts good industries, the kind we want," says Oswaldo Alves. Foreign corporations were among the first to see the advantages; Volvo built a factory, lured in part by the chance to work out improved bus designs with city planners. And new businesses continued to arrive throughout the 1980s, drawn as much by the quality of life for executives fleeing São Paolo as by the ease of doing business with the nearby Southern Cone countries of Argentina and Paraguay. Even in the teeth of Brazil's endless recession and inflation, the number of jobs continued to increase. By 1990 there were 346 factories in the Industrial City, generating fifty thousand direct jobs and one hundred and fifty thousand indirect ones—and 17 percent of the entire state's tax revenue.

The boom in business, the constant rezoning, the speed with which decisions are made—anywhere else in Brazil, and most places in the world, these conditions would have led to corruption on a massive scale. Influence undoubtedly carries some weight in Curitiba: groups of businessmen keep the pressure on to rezone the streets where they have buildings, for instance. But by all accounts the problem is relatively small, as far as I could tell because most people have bought into Lerner's image of the city as a whole. "People do come in to complain," says Liana Vellicelli, the city planner, when asked about it. "A neighborhood politician may say, 'This street is really important. Can you do something for it?' Or someone may say, 'You've put an express bus down my street. I can't live there anymore.' And we say, 'It's for the city.'" The attitude feeds on itself; companies out in the Industrial City, for instance, have begun to fund hundreds of slots in the municipal day-care centers near their plants. And in turn the companies have begun to thrive, Vermont-style, on the city's image, even though that image has been created only in the last two decades. "Our best marketing is to say that we are from Curitiba," one executive told the Brazilian newsmagazine *Veja* last year. "The fact that our product is Curitiban gives it a certain charisma to consumers from other regions," said another.

★ ★ ★

Jaime Lerner is widely and affectionately described as a political naïf; indeed, in 1984, at the end of military rule, he ran in the first democratic elections and was beaten, a victim of vote fraud. Disgusted, he more or less renounced electoral politics and moved to Rio, where he worked as a consultant. (It was in Rio that he dreamed up the tube stations for the buses.) In 1988, however, he decided to run once more for mayor of his hometown. The only problem was, he'd switched his residence to Rio and forgotten to switch it back. He was almost prohibited from running and was not allowed to campaign until ten days before the vote. His sister-in-law, Ester Proveller, remembers that stretch run: "We did almost nothing. It was like Carnaval in those days: everyone brought their old T-shirts out of the closet, made new ones, put up signs. All we did was organize for election day so they wouldn't rob us again. You'd walk through the street in your Jaime shirt and everyone was thumbs up. People would stop their cars and ask, 'Do you have any kind of paper from Mr. Lerner so I can put it in my windshield?'" He won 60 percent of the vote in a crowded field, and his term lasted until 1993; when he left office, his popularity rating was 92 percent.

For all his popularity, though, Lerner's third term was by far the hardest of his career, for it involved a different set of problems— almost a different city. Curitiba had nearly doubled in size since his previous administration; and though some of the growth came from executives arriving to work in Industrial City, most of it came from peasants unable to survive in the countryside. Labor-intensive coffee plantations had been all but replaced by crops like soybeans, which needed only one man on a tractor to cultivate them; one byproduct of this change, as nearly everywhere on earth, was a flood of people to the cities. Curitiba was a natural destination, not just because of proximity but because its reputation as a decent place had begun to spread; as a result, by the early 1990s there were 209 separate slum areas in the city, containing about 176,000 people, or roughly one in nine Curitibans. Because the city is fairly flat, the *favelas* do not stand out like they do in Rio, where they cling to every hillside. Still, the poverty was real enough. One community settled on an old industrial waste site and left, reluctantly, only after municipal officials sank a pipe into the ground and demonstrated that they could fry an egg with the methane that spewed out. The city's morbidity statistics, always a mix of First and Third World diseases, began to show more and more of the infections associated with bad water and rats.

More starkly than in the past, Mayor Lerner, who had created a magnificent city for a poor but by no means destitute population, was facing the kind of challenge faced in cities from New York to Nairobi. He kept his old modus operandi—mornings in street clothes running charettes at his log cabin office on the grounds of a city park, afternoons at city hall dealing with day-to-day needs—but all of a sudden more was riding on the outcome. "The job, it's a job of balancing needs and potentials. If you only work on the big issues, you're far from the people. If you only work on the daily needs, you don't do anything fundamental. *You have to understand you are responsible for the hope of people, their hope for change.* If your city isn't changing, then you're frustrating their hope." In 1989 he was facing quite a bit of frustration and a hell of a lot of hope, which is a scary place for a politician to find himself.

He waded right in, of course. One of the first new programs was called *"Tudo Limpo,"* or "All Clean"; it employs teams of fifteen local residents to clean up their *favelas.* Most of the employees are women, often the single mothers who predominate in the slums. They work for eighty-nine days—under Brazilian law they'd become government employees on the ninetieth day—cutting brush and digging out the ditches that line the unpaved roads. Ester Proveller, who runs the program, took me to visit Vila California, a mixed neighborhood of the sort common to Curitiba, where a small brick-walled house with a car in the driveway might abut a tarpaper shack. The occasional goat grazed along the edge of the road. After a few wrong turns we found the workers, wearing the straw sun hats and the green vests that come with the job, raking and weeding at the top of a hilly section. "Eighteen months ago my husband went out to pay a bill and he didn't come back," says Jeda Silva, hoe in hand. Of her three children, one is mentally retarded. In the last big rains their shack was wrecked; the city program was giving her enough money to eat and to buy wood for her next home. Once a week a social worker comes and sits with the women and talks for an hour or two about problems they're having, about avoiding alcohol, maybe about birth control—though every official winces when I bring up the topic, wary that the Church might take offense. "The classes are a help," says Jeda. Last time she told the social worker that she slept in one bed with her two girls, who are twelve and five. "She told me that wasn't so good, that I should buy a new bed. So that's what

I'll do with my next payment." The paternalism in such programs is undeniable. When a newly arrived peasant gets a mortgage for a low-income house, for instance, the housing authority insists on a counseling session. "We tell them, 'Don't spend your money on liquor,'" a spokesman explains. What makes it seem all right is that it's an *effective* paternalism, not a sham.

That is to say, when Lerner's wife, Fanny, who heads the city's children's programs, says, "We try to do for them like we would for our own children," she actually means it. In 1990 the number of streetchildren in Curitiba had increased to about five hundred—nothing like the tens of thousands that roam the larger cities of Brazil, but clearly heading in that direction. She opened a shelter with activities ongoing all day in an effort to keep the children off the streets. "Not like school, because they won't go to school," she says. "They need a lot of love." And if they don't find it at the shelter, they can go to one of thirteen "support houses," where a pair of houseparents raises eight or ten of the streetchildren. If you want to call them orphanages, I suppose you could; it goes to show that intent and attitude are what really matter. Many boys from the street have been enrolled in the newsvendor program; you see them piling out of trucks at dawn, selling newspapers supplied at a discount by the publisher. They have a dormitory of their own, and half their earnings are saved for them till they are old enough to leave. Other kids, wearing special vests, carry bags for shoppers at the roving street markets that the city sponsors. When the new Botanic Garden was inaugurated a couple of years ago, boys from nearby slums tore up most of the flowerbeds. Instead of posting police, the city hired the children as assistant gardeners.

Two years later the number of streetchildren had dropped to about two hundred. "We know them all by name, and we talk to them constantly, trying to find a program they'll join," says Mrs. Lerner. "The most important thing in the programs is food," she adds—important not just because the kids are hungry, but because all over Brazil children will sniff glue to ward off hunger pangs. "My office spends more on food than on anything else. I remember once my husband came by, and he asked the children, 'What do you like best about the program? Your teacher? The games?' And he was very surprised when they all started shouting, 'The snacks, the snacks.'" When kids are lacking parents, or they're afraid to go home and get beaten again, paternalism is what they need. Food is what they need. Love is what they need. They come out differently if they get it.

The city doesn't wait for kids to become homeless, either. Lerner said from the start of his career that his two priorities were the environment and children, and a large percentage of the municipal budget goes to education, beginning with the city's day-care centers, which are free to children three months or older. The centers run eleven hours a day, allowing parents to get to and from work, and serve three meals and a snack. The federal government runs the elementary and high schools, but in Brazil school lasts only half a day; and even if there were jobs, federal law prohibits Brazilians from working until they're fourteen. So there are long hours to be filled each day. Upper-class kids take music lessons or go to the sports center. Poor kids hang out, or they did until the city inaugurated a system of "PIA" centers—*pia* is Indian slang for small child and also stands for Childhood and Adolescence Integration Program. Christine Braga took me to one of them in a *favela* called Sabara near the Industrial City.

It occupied a typical plot of *favela* land—a steep patch of bare dirt leading to a sour drainage ditch. The slope, however, wasn't eroding away: the twelve- and thirteen-year-old boys in the program, under

the leadership of a grizzled older man named Oswaldo, had planted
bed after bed of vegetable crops in the soil. Onions, lettuce, pars-
ley, tomato, spinach, cabbage, broccoli, pumpkin, popcorn. Orange
trees, tangerine trees. Oswaldo had grown up a peasant farmer
and was passing on to the gang of skinny boys his pleasure in the
work. "They come spontaneously," he says—attendance at the PIA
is voluntary. "But when I explain the importance of the vegetables,
the flowers, and when they see the plants growing, they can know
the importance of their jobs." Sidney, Gilberto, Claudio, Willmar,
Marcio, another Marcio, Allesandro, Lindomar, Fabio, and Gilmar
clustered around me, insisting I take down their names. "They fight
sometimes, especially Lindomar," notes Oswaldo. "I tell them they
have to go home for the day, and that stops it right there." In one
corner of the plot, row after row of potted marigolds sat under black
mesh screening to protect them from the sun. The PIA gets the seed
from the city and in turn sells the flowers back for use in the parks
—the boys make a small amount of money. "My mother is sick and I
want to help support the house," says Claudio. "My grandmother is
trying to build a house," adds Fabio, "and I want to buy some bricks."
Every one of them wore his orange PIA cap, the brims so tattered
they were peeling back. Everyone but Willmar. "Mine's at home—
my mother's washing it today," he explains.

I have been in plenty of places that felt degraded, but this—
though just as poor—felt precisely the opposite. Actively undegrad-
ed. Respected. Cared for. The three-year-olds from the day-care
center came out for a walk, trailing their teacher elephant-style,
hand on the belt of the child in front. Oswaldo started quizzing
them about vegetables. "What kind of onion is this? A red onion.
Who eats onions? All of you!"

A couple of blocks away, a line of women waited outside a tiny community center. A garbage truck had just pulled up, but it wasn't carrying garbage; it was carrying food. For three years now the city has been buying surplus food from farmers in the surrounding countryside and trading it for bags of garbage—six kilos of trash bought a sack of rice, potatoes, beans, and bananas. For a kilo more, some eggs. The program began in 1989 when an outbreak of leptospirosis, a rat-borne disease, was noted in the slums. Because the streets are narrow and unpaved, the garbage trucks hired by the city couldn't get up them to collect trash, which was piling up in the *favelas*. Lerner's team made a few quick calculations: how much would it cost to pay the garbage haulers (a private concern) to collect the trash from the crowded slums? When they had a figure, they determined how much food they could buy for that sum and then let the slumdwellers collect the trash themselves and bring it down out of the *favelas* to the trucks. Along the way, the program manages to support small farmers who might otherwise have to abandon their fields and migrate to town.

The community center in this *favela*—and the 774 families it serves—is run by a shy man named Odair, a shoemaker who had been elected by his neighbors three years in a row. ("I don't say anything at all before the election. People just see the job I've done.") "It's completely changed here from when I arrived in 1989," he says, as we watch people wait for the food to be distributed. It wasn't charity: it was food they'd earned, and it was even nice to hear one woman complain that there hadn't been any honey or garlic in the shipment for weeks. But it was clear that the ticket books, meticulously filled in by Odair when the people brought their garbage to the collection site, were precious possessions. "You are responsible

for this program," reads the text on the ticket book. "Keep on coop-
erating and we will get a cleaner Curitiba, cleaner and more human.
You are an example to Brazil and even to the rest of the world."

*　　　*　　　*

Since many of these people have been evicted from their homes
in the countryside, a house is an urgent need. Not just shelter—
a house they own, on a lot they own. "The most important thing
is the land," says the president of COHAB, the municipal housing
corporation. "When they have the land, it begins to give them . . .
validity," he explains. "They never had any stability before."

Until the mid-1980s, Curitiba had a fairly standard public housing program. It built more units per capita than any other Brazilian
city and did a good job of scattering them around in small pockets
so that they blended in with neighborhoods. But the main source
of funding, the national housing bank, collapsed in 1985. "It went
extinct," says one official: the victim of another of the enormous
scandals that periodically rock the country. At the same time, the
demand for housing skyrocketed as the countryside poured into the
favelas. By 1993 COHAB's waiting list had swelled to fifty-four thousand families; and having very little money, Curitiba had to change
its strategy. Abandoning the policy of small, scattered sites, the
city bought one of the few large plots of land left within its limits, a
swath of farmland bounded by several rivers.

We stood on a rise in this neighborhood—Novo Bairro, or
New Neighborhood, is what it's called—and watched as bulldoz-
ers scraped and contoured the hills. Though city planners had done
their best to leave trees in place, it still looked pretty barren, as if it

was waiting for a few hundred suburban tract homes to go in around pointlessly looping lanes. In fact, though, this cleared field would soon be home to fifty thousand families, perhaps two hundred thousand people. When we turned around on the hilltop, we could see parts of Novo Bairro that had already been sold and occupied; small houses crept like a tidemark across the land, avoiding only the soccer fields around the schools. The city was not building the homes—the landowners were building them, sometimes with the aid of a city mortgage on a small pile of bricks and windows. Every third house seemed to be doubling as a building supply store; and everywhere people plastered, framed, roofed. "Sixty percent of the lower-income people are involved in the construction industry any-how," says one COHAB executive. "They know how to build."

And here is the moving part. With your plot of land comes not only a deed and a pair of trees (one fruit-bearing and one orna-mental), but also an hour downtown with an architect. "The per-son explains what's important to him—a big window out front, or room in the kitchen. They tell how many kids they have, and so on. And then we help draw up a plan," says one architect, who has more than three thousand of "his" homes scattered around the city. "Once we had a plumber who wanted a house that would rotate so it would always be in the sun." That request they couldn't handle, but the day I was there clients lined up clutching magazine pictures of Swiss chalets and suburban-style ranches. The architects did their best to come up with simple designs—and then they num-bered the rooms. "Most people can only afford to build one room at a time, so we show them the logical order to go in," one designer explains. At the moment, in the center of Novo Bairro, COHAB is building "Technology Street," an avenue of twenty-four homes, each built using some different construction technique—bamboo covered with plaster, say—so that people can get ideas for the kind of house they might want. Already you drive through acre after acre of public housing, which is actually private housing, and not one house looks like any of its neighbors. They are all really small, smaller than most Americans would want to live in, but they all say something about the people who built them. "It's a house built out of love," says the housing chief. "And because of that, people won't leave it behind. They're going to consolidate their lives there, become part of the city."

One of the first structures to go up at Novo Bairro was a glass tube bus station, linking this enclave to the rest of the city. "Integration" is a word one hears constantly from official Curitiba, another of its mantras. To American ears it conjures up our national horror, race, but here it means much more. It means knitting together the entire city, rich, poor, and in-between—knitting it together culturally and economically and physically. Hitoshi Nakamura, a native of Osaka, is the city parks commissioner and one of Lerner's longtime collaborators. "We have to have communication with the people of the slums," he said one day as we were talking about the problems posed by settlers invading fragile bottomlands along the rivers. "If we don't, if they start to feel like *favelados,* then they will go against the city. Before they feel like *favelados,* we must get there and implant these programs. If we give them attention, they don't feel abandoned. They feel like citizens." The truth of his diagnosis can be seen in Curitiba's largest and oldest *favela,* Vila Pinto, a dense knot of perhaps five thousand people along one of the main highways. It grew for many years without anyone really doing anything to help it, and now it has a different feel from the more recent slums along the periphery—it has acquired its own culture, sullen and insular. I drove through one day in an unmarked police car with two narcotics detectives; though it was midafternoon, all the young men who saw us coming ducked away into alleys. "If you read the tabloid papers, every day there's a story from Vila Pinto—something with a knife," says one Curitiban.

More than most places, though, Curitiba has managed to follow Mayor Lerner's dictum: "When you have a city with ghettos—ghettos of poor or of rich—then it's not a city." Housing is surprisingly mixed: there are a few gated condominium communities, but there are also expensive new homes going up not far from hovels. Partly it's self-interest. "If you're rich, you need that type of people—they're your domestics, maybe," says one housing planner, trying to explain why there was little not-in-my-backyard outcry when the city began new public housing developments.

Still, in the early 1980s (the same years when American cities began to notice an upsurge in homelessness), signs of a backlash began to emerge. The new arrivals to Curitiba often tried to earn a living selling from small pushcarts. "It was a problem for the merchants, and a problem for the streets," says Liana Vellicelli, the planner. "We thought about it—we couldn't just say, 'Go away.' This is their job. If the city can't offer them other jobs, we have to do what we can to make this work." The government asked the vendors to form an association and began discussions with the leaders. They selected spots where they were interested in selling—plazas, say, where business was good, or particular bus terminals. And then their joint committee set up a schedule, so that a street market could rotate through each of these spots every week or two. "Instead of ceding permanent areas for street markets—which would have to be a long way from prime zones—why not concede better areas during specified days and hours?" asks Lerner. "It's an invasion, but controlled, consented, and regular. We integrate not only by the administration of physical space but through the administration of time." And it works. The city designed simple, portable stalls for vendors and gave them licenses. "People used to be afraid of these sellers," says Vellicelli. "Now they have a number, they're a part of the city."

Over the long run, real integration will require real education, giving newer, poorer residents a shot at the jobs being created in the Industrial City. "We found when we talked to the executives, that they were hiring labor from São Paulo," says Ester Proveller, who oversees the job training program. "They said Curitibans weren't well trained. We were surprised at first, because it's supposed to be a very modern city. But because of that, it attracts a lot of people who don't have any skills—people who are used to planting." Around the same time that Proveller was doing her survey, she noticed that Curitiba had decided to modernize its bus fleet. "I had the idea to turn the old ones into classrooms," she says. "Jaime said yes right away, and he came up with the name: *Linha do Ofício*," or Line to Work. She began with six buses, which were gutted and refitted as classrooms for small-motor repair, typing, hairdressing, and other skills businesses said they needed. The buses were driven to various poor neighborhoods and parked for three months, the length of a course. "We tried to make the classrooms look nice, to attract people—the ones we deal with are ones who don't want to be going to school, so it helps that it's in a bus," she explains. The courses aren't completely free: three months tuition is two bus tokens, or about seventy cents: "we understand that if you pay for something you value it more."

We stopped at one location in the Boa Vista neighborhood, where a classroom bus sat a block from the bus terminal. Its destination sign read *"Datilografia"* (typing), and inside there were fifteen students hunched over manual typewriters learning the keyboard. One young man, his hands covered with a cloth to keep him from peeking, typed a lesson from the municipal textbook:

> When you feel like crying, call me
> So I can cry with you
> When you feel like smiling, tell me
> So we can smile together
> But when you don't need me, tell me so
> So I can look for someone else.

At the next machine, a fourteen-year-old girl worked on a business letter: "Senhor Prefeito: We have the satisfaction to say we received your letter from his Excellency . . ." A list of rules was posted at the front of the bus: they had been drawn up by the class at its first session and included warnings that anyone who came late twice or missed two classes would be kicked out. "In some neighborhoods they say, 'Don't bring your knife' and 'You can't smoke marijuana on the bus,'" says Ester cheerfully. Beneath the list of rules stood a few brooms, and when class ends the students used them to clean up before vacating the bus to the next group of would-be typists, who were already sitting on the curb next to the bus.

Curitiba sponsors a kind of higher education designed to integrate the city, too. In 1990 Lerner announced plans for an Open University of the Environment. Three months later it was complete, a string of classrooms spiraling up out of an abandoned stone quarry and built almost entirely out of old telephone poles. "It was awful, this place," says Cleon Santos, the university's rector; it was a dangerous sinkhole dragging down an entire neighborhood. Now people flock there on weekends to feed the swans and walk up the ramp for a peek out of the quarry's crater at the surrounding city. (Needless to say, the surrounding land has gone up in value.) During the week smaller crowds arrive to take a free, basic course about the thinking behind the city's evolution—about how the parks came into being and why the zoning map looks the way it does. Though anyone can come, the city seeks out "opinion-makers" to invite and modifies the course for their needs. "With teachers, we talk about the historical aspects; we talk about the scientific fundamentals of ecology; we talk about where they might take their classes around the city," says Santos. "With taxi drivers, we emphasize the reasons for our transit system. They're upset by the good buses because they lose customers, so we have a section about the historical sites where they could take tourists."

Santos's faculty is also establishing a database about Curitiba: information on air quality, on income levels, on the thousand other facts that together compose the profile of a city. The information is hard to come by at the moment; the planning institute, for instance, works with ten-year-old data on disease and morbidity because the federal government ran out of money for censuses. "Once we've got a baseline, we'll be able to make sure things aren't getting worse," he says.

A stack of leaflets from the latest city improvement campaign sat on Santos's desk. This crusade encouraged people not to blow their car horns so much. I asked him what big issues are left to deal with here. "The quality of life is good here," he said thoughtfully. "If you ask me what to do this very moment to make it better, I don't know what to say."

★   ★   ★

It's indeed possible that Curitiba may have broken the back of its social problems. Though the population will continue to grow steadily— by 2020, according to one estimate, the city will add another million people—the pace should slow. "There just aren't that many people left to come from the countryside," maintains the director of the city's housing authority. "It's pretty empty out there now."

But the American experience would indicate that growth and poverty are not the only problems cities face, that affluence can sap a society as well. Urban areas can turn stale and uninteresting: at best neutral ground for making money, not attractive enough to counteract the gravitational force of the suburbs. That seems unlikely to happen in Curitiba, as long as officials continue to ask the two questions we Westerners feel constrained from asking: What is a community for? And what is a person for?

We can't bring ourselves to ask them because the answer is supposed to be that people will decide for themselves what is best for them. Out of this cacophony of individual choices a sweet symphony is supposed to emerge, but in fact much of North America is silent: people kept a hundred yards apart by the size of their suburban estates, watching TV (often in separate rooms), almost afraid to mix. One survey found three-quarters of Americans did not know their next-door neighbors. Almost inevitably, this kind of society consumes to excess. Unable to take our pleasure in community, in contact with other people, we seek our solace in things. Not concerts but compact discs, not football in the park but football on TV.

"I know it's the right of people to live where they want," says Lerner. "If you want to live in a condominium of wealthy people, that's okay." And indeed some Curitibans do, building big houses behind gates with guards. But government—democracy—needn't stop there. "You can also offer an option for people who want to live more . . . gregariously," says Lerner.

"You have to have a certain kind of complicity with people when you're trying to understand what are their problems, what are their dreams. People, they are not living in the city just for survival. You have to love the city. They have to have this *relationship* that has to do with identity, with a sense of belonging." Sometimes even great bus service or nice schools are not the key. "There are some *bairros* that don't have those facilities, and the people are happy. Why? Because their father lived there; their grandfather lived there. There's a sense of belonging to a place."

Creating that kind of identity, instilling whatever it is that keeps people from giving their lives over to gangs or to shopping malls, in a city that's tripling in size over two decades is far from easy. It's one reason Lerner has focused so intently on children, whose relation to the world is still unformed, still up for grabs. "In the place where children are happy, you can understand you're in a good way. They have to feel safe; they have to have a certain opportunity; they have to have a sense of equality, of being the equal of everyone—it doesn't matter if their parents are migrants." He begins to speak again of his own childhood in his father's store, helping peasants without socks try on pairs of shoes. "When I was at university, I would wake up at 5:00 A.M. and have coffee in the same shop with the workers of the railroad. I came to understand what people wanted, I think. Trying to interpret a collective dream, a collective desire—it's very difficult."

So difficult that in our country (and in most of Brazil and much of the world) we've simply given up, accepted that life will take place in an ever more private realm. Mike Davis, in *City of Quartz*, his sweeping history of Los Angeles, describes the "destruction of public space"—the transformation of a "once-upon-a-time demiparadise of free beaches, luxurious parks," and other "genuinely democratic spaces" into a pay-as-you-go world of malls where bathrooms are for patrons only, neighborhoods are isolated against criminals (and everyone else) by concrete barriers, and "security guard" is the fastest-growing occupation. Libraries close at midday, replaced by access to the information superhighway for those who can afford it. Not long ago, visiting friends in a Massachusetts suburb, our host took our daughter to the playground—which turned out to be an elaborate jungle gym installed in a mall and charging five bucks a head. (It doesn't take much political insight to figure out how much longer the city where it is located will maintain its public playgrounds.) In such a world, "politician" becomes a curseword; trained by the Reagan years to despise things public and to worship the "private sector," we cannot begin to grapple with problems, including almost every environmental challenge, that clearly require government to be a major player.

But scolding people, or hectoring them with slogans, can't redeem politics. Telling citizens to ride the bus for the sake of the environment only works if the bus works. The only slogan I saw painted on a wall in Curitiba was not a slogan at all, but a poem, by

Paolo Leminski, one of the city's great literary figures. It was three stories up, near the center of town, directly above the small municipal poetry store. Inelegantly translated, it reads: "Let the pleasure of the sheer perception of your senses be the critic of reason."

I set out one day on the bike path that ran by my apartment, intent on compiling a sensory catalogue of a little of the urban pleasure Curitiba offered. (The 150-kilometer *ciclovia* network, inaugurated during the second administration, was Oswaldo Alves's idea. "Riding bikes was still in the memory of the city, but people had given it up because it was too dangerous," he explained.) On this sunny afternoon, the path was crowded with cyclists, but most were just noodling along; and it was no problem to push my baby daughter in her stroller. The path ran beside the Rio Belém; the water was dirty and carried some trash, but even two blocks from downtown, flowering trees were growing wild out over the banks. We walked by a sandy soccer field jammed with eight-year-old boys (not a parent in sight) and then across a street and into the Bosque de Papa, a small park dedicated to Pope John Paul II, who visited Curitiba on his last trip to Brazil. Cobbled paths wound through the park to a small cluster of wood-plank buildings: a replica of a Polish immigrant village that was moved here when the park was commissioned. One building, a chapel with four rows of pews, holds a beautiful icon of the black virgin of Czechostowa. Outside, older women sat on benches watching their grandchildren play. The path left the park and moved into a residential neighborhood of big and small houses, running past a concrete municipal skateboard ramp that would shake the heart of any city attorney in the United States. Young trees grew all along the edge of the sidewalk, carefully staked out by city workers—it's easy to see there will be a corridor of shade in another decade. Past a Bavarian beer house and a bike-rental stand, the path reached the Parque São Lourenço, whose big lake was one of the original flood-control projects. On the right a municipal go-cart ramp plummeted down from the highest hill. On the left a shepherd gathered the municipal herd of sheep, which were done trimming the grass for the day. Swans and geese floated on the lake; at its head sat the former glue factory, now the municipal Creativity Center, with a ceramics studio, a sculpture garden, and a giant chess set with pieces the size of children. The *ciclovia* connects eventually with the other parks—Parque Barrigui, for instance, where today Ziggy Marley was giving an outdoor concert, the Third Age center (for seniors) was holding quiet yoga sessions, and remote-control planes were whizzing around the municipal remote-control airplane range.

The next morning I headed downtown toward the pedestrian mall, stopping at the Passeio Público, the city's original park, to eat a big meal for a couple of dollars at the outdoor restaurant. This is no Tavern-on-the-Green: a raucous samba band was performing at one end of the open restaurant, and I could hear its music even after I'd finished my lunch and left on a stroll down the middle of the Rua Quinze. Ritzy stores sit next to cheap and crowded *lanchonetes* on this pedestrian mall, and hardware stores with a thousand pots hanging from the ceiling stand next to booksellers. A parade of chanting Evangelicals suddenly appeared at one end of the street; they had dressed one of their number as Jesus and were carrying him on a sedan chair down the street. There was a volleyball court in one of the central plazas, half a dozen playgrounds, and lottery salesmen bellowing on every corner. One of the roving markets had taken root near a bus terminal, and I recognized many of the handicrafts from my tour of the adult education centers. People wandering out of the main cathedral after noontime mass blinked to be back in the sun. A man dressed as a giant molar gave a lecture on oral hygiene from a stage while dozens of dental assistants in their white uniforms handed out leaflets and demonstrated proper brushing. In a military tent set up under some flowering *ipé* trees, an army doctor showed a video about AIDS. Waiters in uniforms—old men—served lunch at the Scheffer deli, an establishment so beloved that when it burned a few years ago the city subsidized its restoration. Card tables from several political parties offered competing anticorruption publications; around every news kiosk, knots of people stood reading the posted front pages. The jacarandas shaded the toucans in the small zoo, and off on one corner a little amusement park offered a ferris wheel and a merry-go-round.

It is a true place, a place full of serendipity. It is not dangerous or dirty; if it was, people would go to the shopping mall instead. It is as alive as any urban district in the world: poems pasted on telephone poles, babies everywhere. The downtown, though a shopping district, is not a money-making machine. It is a habitat, a place for *living*—the exact and exciting opposite of a mall. A rich and diverse and *actual* place that makes the American imitations—the South Street Seaports and Faneuil Hall Marketplaces—seem like the wan and controlled re-creations that they are.

I had to remind myself, wandering through Curitiba, that all this spontaneity didn't happen by itself—that without the planning and the risky gambles that created the conditions for it to evolve, the center would likely be dangerous and dying. There is one subtle reminder every Saturday morning. Municipal workers roll out huge sheets of paper down the middle of one of the central blocks of the pedestrian mall and set out pots of paint so that hundreds of kids can—without knowing what they're doing—re-create the sit-in that drove away the cars and launched this pleasure-filled street at the beginning of Lerner's first term. Some of these children are undoubtedly the offspring of children who were brought here that first dramatic Saturday, and their presence raises a question of the first importance: Can you, by changing the conditions under which people live, slowly change the character of the people? It's a key question; any long-term hope for dealing with the massive problems of the environment involves changing people around the world. Or no—not *changing* them. Bringing out the *part* of them that responds to nonmaterial pleasures like painting on the sidewalk and walking in a crowd and gossiping on a bench and drinking a beer at a bar. And slowly deemphasizing the side that we know all too well: the private, muffled grabbiness, the devotion to comfort, the fear of contact that resides in each of us, side by side with the qualities we need to muster.

Curitiba is an interesting test case, for its people, by all accounts, are not naturally gregarious. Lerner is the exception; the rule, says novelist Cristavao Tezza, who moved to Curitiba at the age of six, is a certain timidity and introversion. "Carnaval is never much of a success here," he says. "It's sort of something forced on us. If you had a classical music festival, it would be much closer to our sense of being." The European influence—especially the lingering mark of the Germans, who were Curitibas' earliest masters—outweighs any Latin tug, he maintains; and it is clearly true that unlike the rest of Brazil, which sways, Curitiba walks in a straight line.

"Curitiba has always been a very tight city," adds another writer, Valencio Xavier. "When someone invites you to his house, you know he wasn't born here. When we were living in São Paulo, we had people in the house constantly. When we moved back here, my wife was shocked—no one invited us over. My neighbor came up to me and said 'You have all these guests in your house, this is very expensive.' He wouldn't let his daughter come visit here because he thought some of our friends were hippies."

Changing something as stubborn as the character of a town takes more than one mayor, even if he serves three terms. But everyone I talk to agrees that Lerner has made a start. "In the last few years this place is different," says Xavier. "Lerner did things that had never happened here before: he put people on the street. In Curitiba things had always happened within four walls. He obliged us to walk. He had these street fairs; he made parks. Before we were like oysters that crack open just a little bit to get the world passing by. Now we are opening up."

Not totally, of course. "In some ways we remain spectators of the town," says Tezza. "I went to a rock show in the old part of town. It was an amazing spectacle—lights, lasers, stroboscopes. But people were just standing and watching. They didn't know if it was okay to dance." Still, says Tezza, it is strange to see how popular Lerner had become. "One of our characteristics was always that we were very critical. We even have a place—the Boca Maldita—where the men just sit all day saying nasty things about people. So Lerner's a phenomenon."

Simply coming to take the pleasures of the city for granted may be the most important—change coming to believe that they will be there, that it is possible to plan your life around the essential decency of a place. One small but telling example: Oswaldo Alves, Lerner's longtime colleague, said that when they were doing the blitzkrieg makeover of the Rua Quinze, they knew people would pick the flowers they were planting all over the street. "We had a huge supply on hand; and the second someone picked them, we'd plant some new ones. We did it day after day, and it wasn't long before people figured out the best place for the flowers was the street." Indeed, Rua Quinze is now better known as Rua das Flores.

Anibal Tacla, a fabric merchant with two stores along the pedestrian mall, remembers the day the new street went in; his father was one of the storeowners sure that the plan would bankrupt him, "that the quality of the people who came to walk here would decrease, that pickpockets would take the place over." Instead, of course, business boomed. With the streets crowded, there was relatively little crime. "All of this is possible because the people of Curitiba now think they live in a First World city," he says. "This message was inbred in us by Jaime Lerner. We're proud to live in Curitiba, and we want to show we can live like grownups." The shopkeepers along the mall had recently formed a trade association, collecting dues so they could advertise jointly and sponsor activities. "In any other part of Brazil, if you talk to a merchant and ask him to pay three hundred dollars a month for an association, he will give you a big four letter word. Here, eighty percent joined up. Everything's like that here now—if you talk to Curitibans about separating their garbage, they will do it, because they know they live in a different city. This mind-condition—it's very important, and it's the exact reverse of what happened in Rio."

But the most impressive transformation may be the willingness of people to support social programs. In a city widely described as conservative, I met no one who thought the city was spending too much money helping the poor: the mixing and contact spurred by all of Lerner's various schemes, and the fact that the schemes work, seems to have lessened the fear and contempt that hobbles such work in other places. "Last Christmas I went out to the lines where people exchange trash for food," recalls Lerner. "And I noticed, out of the corner of my eye, a guy I knew from architecture school, carrying a sack of garbage. I didn't say anything, but pretty soon he called me over. And he said, 'I know what you're thinking, I'm not in a bad situation. I'm here with my kids because I want them to understand the importance of this.'"

★   ★   ★

When Melani Krishnankutty, a Berkeley graduate student researching the city, arrived in 1993 to intern at IPPUC, the city's planning institute, she found that many of the city's top planners couldn't tell her what bus to take home: "they wouldn't dream of coming to work without their cars. They love the car, and they talk about what a great driving city it is, since there are so few cars on the street." Not every Curitiban has been transformed; this is a success story, but it takes place in the real world.

Krishnankutty distributed questionnaires to junior planners throughout the city, and many of them responded with complaints: too much of the character of the city was concentrated downtown, and the neighborhoods of the periphery have not been as carefully thought out; changing traffic patterns have rerouted cars through residential neighborhoods; many people still worked a great distance from their houses. Other respondents, especially among the younger planners who had joined the city in recent years, thought Curitiba paid too much attention to marketing: several dismissed as "propaganda" the current slogan, "The Ecological City." "Sometimes they laugh when they see people coming from outside to visit Curitiba," says Krishnan-kutty. "They say, 'Wow, the hype is incredible.'"

Some of the problems are more than skin-deep, insoluble with the usual mix of cleverness and frugality because they involve human greed and hopelessness. When the city began recycling, the assumption was that it would help Curitiba's poorest of the poor, the "cartpeople" who tow their loads of scrap paper and glass around town like human donkeys. The plan was to let them pick up most of the recyclables left by the curb: the city installed only a token separation plant of its own—thinking that, with all the publicity about recycling, the junkmen would find a higher volume of scrap on the street and that now they'd be able to get at the paper and tin without rummaging through the coffee grounds, because it would be in separate bags. Even more important, there was a plan to form them into an association that would allow them to deal from a position of strength with the private companies that bought the scrap. Indeed, several people I spoke to in Curitiba assured me that this had happened, and one of the many booklets I was given, "Curitiba: Toward an Environmentally Correct City," announced that these cooperatives had allowed the cartpeople to triple their income.

In reality, the Association of Small Pushcarts is run from a narrow fenced lot across the highway from the Vila Pinto slum, a lot strewn with mounds of mineral water bottles and drifts of broken glass. Rubens Ferraira, a powerfully built man in a baseball cap, led us to a small office with a couple of battered chairs, sat down, and with some prodding began to tell the real story of this cooperative. Vila Pinto has plenty of cartpeople, he said—six or eight hundred people in the slum earn their living pulling the carts. But very few of them come to his lot with their trash; virtually all continue to sell their findings to six big entrepreneurs on the edge of town, who form a monopoly able to manipulate prices. One cart might gather three hundred kilos of paper a day, Ferraira said. If he could sell it at its real value—about eight cruzeiros per kilo—he could clear twenty-four hundred cruzeiros a day, or the equivalent of about ten dollars. Not much, but a life. Instead, the big entrepreneurs offer about three cruzeiros, the equivalent of four dollars a day, which is poverty of the abject kind.

So why do they sell to the private companies? "They know they're being ripped off," says Ferraira. "But the entrepreneur provides the cart, which the man has to have. And he lives in a small shelter provided by the entrepreneur." It may not be much of a house—"there might be seven families living in ten meters by twenty," says Ferraira—but it's a house. The cartpeople live so close to the edge that they have no way to survive a month or two until higher profits accumulate and they can find a new home. "You have to pay him tonight so he can eat tomorrow," says Ferraira. And the city has also failed to find the money for modern equipment for Ferraira's scrap lot. His old paper press can handle a ton a day, compared with ten tons an hour at the big private plants. He spends half an hour showing me the various scams the private companies run to take money from the carters. Computer paper is worth twice the price of regular stock, for instance, but the entrepreneurs will simply announce there's no market for it and pay the regular price. A kind name for the whole arrangement would be "involuntary servitude"; "slavery" is not as obvious a hyperbole as it should be. But it would take more than the city's brand of everyone's-a-winner optimism to raise up these poorest of the poor: it would take cash, and it would take a willingness to confront powerful men. For the moment, the carters remain a constant visible reminder that this shining city on a hill still casts a shadow.

Nevertheless, as the cloth merchant Anibal Tacla points out, Curitiba suffers from high aspirations. "It's true we have some people asking for dollars in the street. But this is similar in the First World, too. I went to Germany recently, and it was much worse. No economy can absorb all the misery around it," especially an economy as terminal as Brazil's.

When I lived in New York City, I spent much of my time writing about homelessness and helped open a small shelter for the homeless. It was the beginning of that crisis—a crisis long since ended, not because there are any fewer homeless people, but because everyone got used to them and would be amazed if there *weren't* families huddled in half the subway stations in the city. By any comparison, Curitiba has worked miracles. "It rains a lot, the streets are slippery, and drivers still go through red lights," reported *Veja*, the Brazilian newsweekly, in its big story on Curitiba's three hundredth anniversary. "Its virtues, however, are unbeatable."

The transit system provides a midterm exam for the city, a snapshot of how far it's come in changing the nature of the city. Not just the efficiency of the transit system, which is world class, but the respect in which it's held—a respect that can be measured in several concrete ways. The bus system relies on terminals, for instance, that allow passengers to switch easily from one line to another. The terminals are open at either end so that the buses can drive in and out; it would be a simple matter to walk in and out without paying, since there's only one guard in a booth and since even the thirty-cent fare represents a hefty share of the minimum wage. Having lived in an infinitely richer city that needed to experiment with pepper sprays to keep young people from sucking up tokens with their mouths after they'd been placed in the fare box, a city where the change clerk sits inside a bulletproof booth and speaks through a microphone, a city where no bus driver would even consider carrying change—having lived in Manhattan, I of course asked about farebeaters. "When you respect the people, they respect you," says Oswaldo Alves, the planner. "The people saw that the municipality was doing a lot for them, and began to take some responsibility."

In 1990, twenty years after Lerner's first inauguration, the speedybus was about to go into service; and the architects sat down to draw the final designs for the tube stations. They eventually decided to build them out of glass, the cheapest and most beautiful material. "They are fragile," says Alves. "But by now people are used to respecting the city. We knew they had that level of respect." Traveling around the city by bus, I saw only one station with broken windows. It was in one of the richest parts of town, right across from the offices of the governor; several people told me the vandalism was a political trick by his forces, designed to make the mayor look bad. Everywhere else the tube stations gleamed clean and unbroken, busy with people on their way out to see the city.

★   ★   ★

When mayors and city planners gathered in Curitiba for an urban conference the week before Rio's 1992 Earth Summit, they produced a document called the Curitiba Commitment. It was full of the usual boilerplate beloved by the UN, vague calls to solve all the problems of all the cities as soon as possible. And it raised the nagging question of whether the city's success is replicable—either in Brazil or in the rest of the world—or whether it's the product of a unique combination of historical circumstance, civic character, and the boundless imagination of Jaime Lerner.

Lerner's years in Rio, where he served as a consultant to the local government, were an education in frustration—even though much of the nation was already aware of his abilities. "You understand how anxious I would get, knowing we had these ideas and no ways to make the decisions," he says. It would be hard to pick a more frustrating country to try and reform: the corruption is so endemic that barely a year after President Fernando Collor de Mello was thrown out of office, thirty of the senators who threw him out were under investigation. (One contended that he had acquired an enormous bank account on his legislator's salary by winning the lottery 250 times, a feat he attributed to the intervention of the Blessed Virgin.) Local leaders are just as out of control. In one state the governor shot another politician point-blank in the head—but since the legislature refused to lift his immunity, he was not arrested. In another the wife of the strongman takes Imelda-style shopping trips to Miami and tells the press "the poor have just as much right to see me looking pretty as anyone else."

The explosion of attention on the grand and petty corruption may be set to shake Brazilian politics in ways that could boost Lerner's career and spread his ideas. Says Cristavao Tezza, the Curitiban novelist, a decade of declining living standards is finally taking its toll. "There's a certain social awareness growing on the part of the intelligent elite. We're starting to realize that Brazil is becoming unsustainable, that there's a growing risk of something occurring by force. So part of the political elite is now geared toward solving real problems." Probably as a result, Lerner's stock is soaring. He's been elected governor of Paraná state, and his phone rings regularly with calls from Brasília, the nation's capital. "There are a lot of people looking for a third way, a way around the traditional parties," says one political aide. Lerner, for his part, would relish the chance if it ever came. His thinking is not confined to cities: he whipped out a pen one day and drew me some sketches of his RURBANS—way stations between the fields and the cities for migrating peasants, where they could spend a generation working in an urban area but still tending a few acres of land. "Being integrated more slowly, so they are not overwhelmed, nor the city," he explains.

To learn from Curitiba, the rest of the world would have to break some long-standing habits—the habit of finding answers in the rich countries, for instance. "People can't imagine there's a city in Brazil with all the facilities," says the director of the city's housing authority. "When I visit America, people are convinced that when I come home, I have to take a jeep from the airport through the jungle, like Tarzan." Residents of the First World "say, 'Curitiba is a Third World city, what can it teach us?'" sighs Lerner. "People in the Third World say, 'We're a First World city.'"

The hardest habit to break, in fact, may be what Lerner calls the "syndrome of tragedy, of feeling like we're terminal patients." Many cities have "a lot of people who are specialists in proving change is not possible. What I try to explain to them when I go to visit is that it takes the same energy to say why something can't be done as to figure out how to do it." Curitiba, he says, is "not a model but a reference," more important as a reservoir of directions and of hope. "I'm sure of one thing. When people come to visit, they won't forget. Because it's a very strong place. I realize there's very few examples in the world. It's hard to make it happen, and that's why it's so strong. For those who make their living selling complexity, it's very strong. For those who want a small sign that it's possible, it's very strong, too."

I was rushing to catch a flight back home when I talked with Lerner for the last time, and I thought to myself that I would miss this city greatly—not only because of its buses and parks, but because in weeks of doing interviews I'd met very few cynics. The resigned weariness of Westerners about government, which leaves only fanatics and hustlers running for office, had lifted from this place. I came of age during Watergate, and so I needed a reminder that politics in its largest sense can actually be a noble and useful profession, can actually change a place and its people. I needed a reminder that "public" is not a notion consigned to the trash heap of history. I needed this month in the middle of a city to think clearly about the villages and forests of my home.

As I was gathering up my papers to leave for the airport, Lerner talked about his most recent trip to New York, where his daughter is a dancer. Though he was attending a conference, he managed to go to ten movies in ten days, not to mention concerts, bars, restaurants. He behaves, apparently, as if every city was a Curitiba; and it is hard not to think that he might be able to create them wholesale by sheer force of exuberant personality. He is, among other things, a passionate devotee of klezmer music, and spent several hours at an outdoor bandshell on the Lower East Side waiting through rock bands to hear a performance by the Klezmatics. (He later invited them to Curitiba, where they were a big hit.) I asked him again about the example Curitiba offers the rest of the world. "The more you study your own condition, the deeper you get in your own reality, the more universal you are," he answered. "Tolstoy said, 'If you want to be universal, sing your village.' This is true in literature, it's true in music—if you know klezmer, you know all of music. And it's true in cities, too. You have to know your village and you have to love it."

Chapter 3
KERALA

In that earliest dawn, before I could make out even the nearest
trees, the sounds were already sharp: roosters crowing and
wild birds starting to sing; the occasional belch of a cow;
and the steady, nasal music that came from a loudspeaker by the
Hindu temple two miles distant. The music rose like a column of
smoke from a chimney, always there but never obscuring the other
sounds—the occasional splash as someone upended a bucket for a
morning shower, the infrequent cough of a car motor. As the sun
came up, I could see more clearly down the valley—could see the
tops of endless coconut and banana palms, a rich green carpet with
here and there a bit of emerald rice paddy showing through. It looked
almost like jungle; it seemed unlikely there were people enough to
be making all that noise.

I had flown out of a harsh Northeast winter to reach this most
tropical tip of India, leaving behind ice-frosted hemlocks for nod-
ding palms, leaving behind the freeze-cleaned air of home for the
pungent vapor of the tropics. My first morning there, jetlagged, I
rose before the sun and stood in my shirtsleeves in the eighty-degree

darkness and wondered if the warm weather was the only thing I'd get from my trip. Or if there was something this most foreign of spots could teach me about my home.

As I started to walk on the well-packed trails through the woods, I saw how carefully the groves were spaced and tended: the trunk of each rubber tree delicately wounded, dripping its thin trickle of white latex into a small saucer; the base of each palm mounded against erosion. Just as the sun pushed above the canopy of fronds, I came out on the dikes that circled and crossed the paddy fields. In one of the small fields seven men bent over sickles, harvesting one handful at a time the stalks of rice. Farther on, in a field already cut, two men hoed the heavy mud, readying it for the next planting. In a ditch along the field's edge, a woman anchored coconut leaves beneath the water with rocks, as a grazing cow looked on. In a few months the leaves would be ready to use as roofing. A steady stream of people walked the dike in the cool of the morning, most with baskets on their heads: rice seedlings, bundles of palm fronds, piles of dried white coconut.

A particular thrill ran through me as I strolled. "This is what the world looks like," I found myself saying. This is one of the two or three archetypal human scenes: rice fields and palm trees, muscled labor, brown skin. It is a dangerous thrill, an inch away from the sentimental gawking that used to send tour buses down the Bowery as guides prattled about the Street of Broken Dreams. Admiring the Taj Mahal, icon of tourist India, is safe—it's a perfect distillation of the extraordinary. But admiring the ordinary, with a passport and a return ticket in your knapsack, verges on the mawkish. Especially in such a poor place—$330 per person per year, on average. Surely the beauty of this valley was a Hobbesian beauty, a gloss over lives short and nasty, insecure and ignorant, primitive and diseased. And surely my attraction was the international equivalent of slumming, a jet-age flapper cabbing up to Harlem to gaze enchantedly on how natural the people seemed.

In part, that's the truth. Kerala *is* poor, even for India, with a per capita income about one-seventieth the American average. But in Kerala the truth is more complicated than in most other places. Expectation and assumption are bent and refracted, neat categories of First World and Third World eroded. On the ground, at least at first glance, Kerala looks little different from the rest of the subcontinent that is home to a fifth of the world. Using the geography of statistics, however, it stands out like Nepal on a relief map.

Consider the most basic human phenomena. The average life expectancy for a North American male is seventy-two years. The average life expectancy for a Keralite male is seventy years. That is to say, a boy born in America this year can expect to die in 2067, while a boy born in Kerala would, actuarially, expire in 2065.

After the most recent in a long series of literacy campaigns, the United Nations recently certified Kerala as 100 percent literate; your chances of having an informed conversation with a passerby are at least as high in Kerala as in Kansas.

Kerala's birth rate, meanwhile, is eighteen per thousand, compared with sixteen per thousand in the United States—and it's falling faster than ours is.

Demographically, in other words, Kerala mirrors the United States on about one-seventieth the cash. In countries of comparable income, and in other states of India, male life expectancy is fifty-eight years and only half the people (and perhaps a third of the women) can read and write; the birth rate hovers around forty per thousand.

Kerala's bizarre success has come despite daunting odds. Only a few spots on earth are as crowded. Kerala squeezes the population of Canada into an area the size of Vancouver Island; with 1,933 people per square mile, it's more than twice as crowded as India as a whole. Not even the diversity of its population—60 percent Hindu, 20 percent Muslim, and 20 percent Christian, a recipe for chronic low-grade warfare in the rest of India—has slowed its progress.

What's more, Kerala's dedication to equality could not have been predicted even a century ago, when caste divided the Hindu population more profoundly than anywhere else in India. The reformer Swami Vivekananda described it as a "lunatic asylum"; one British officer called Kerala "the most oppressive and rack-rented region on the face of the earth."

Most unlikely of all, of course, is that it has achieved what it has while staying poor. Extremely poor. There are disputes about the state's precise per capita income: some economists say remittances from foreign workers may raise it 10 or 15 percent; others argue that cash goes further in its markets. But there can be no doubt about its very real poverty. New Jersey anthropologist Richard Franke, the Westerner who has observed Kerala most carefully and on whose accounts I have drawn heavily, recently studied 170 families in the small village of Nadur. "Many do not even own beds," he reports. Forty-two percent had only cooking utensils, a wooden bench, and a few stools. That is the sum of their possessions. Thirty-six percent had some chairs and cots, and 19 percent actually had a table. In five households he found cushioned seats, dressers, and the like. There was one VCR, one refrigerator, and one television—all in the same home. Romanticizing Kerala is a mistake. Its people want and need more than they have. They are too poor.

But there is risk, too, in *not* romanticizing this story, in not under-
scoring just how remarkable it is. In the tropical regions of northeast
Brazil, about as far below the equator as Kerala is above it, and in
a place with somewhat greater per capita income, an anthropologist
named Nancy Scheper-Hughes recently wrote a book called *Death
Without Weeping: The Violence of Everyday Life*. It is filled with stories
of dead babies and endless pregnancies, of typhoid and polio and
bubonic plague, of every possible kind of degradation, oppression, and
dysfunction—where "the goal is not resistance but simply existence."
The same could be said of a hundred other regions spread across Africa, South America, Eastern Europe, and Asia—and indeed of many
communities, rural and urban, in the United States. By contrast,
Franke could title his most recent book about Kerala *Life Is a Little
Better*. He cites a "physical quality of life index," or PQLI—a compos-
ite statistic running on a scale from zero to a hundred that combines
many basic indicators of human well-being. By 1981 Kerala's score of 82
far exceeded all of Africa; in Asia only the incomparably richer South
Korea (85), Taiwan (87), and Japan (98) ranked higher. By 1988 Kerala's score had risen to 88—compared with an all-India total of 60.

Again, Kerala—even by Indian standards—is not rich, rank-
ing near the middle of the country's twenty-two states in per capita
income. This contradiction can't be repeated too often: it undercuts
so many maxims that we consider true, consider almost intuitive.
Richer people are healthier; richer people live longer; richer people
have more opportunity for education. Richer people have fewer children. In order to improve human lives we need large-scale economic
growth. In this sense it is a more remarkable place even than Curitiba. Jaime Lerner has taken a tough hand and played it brilliantly;
Kerala has changed the rules of the game entirely.

So it was the natural next stop on my journey. Foreign as it was in every way—hot weather, hot food—I needed its example to think more boldly about my home place. Curitiba had redeemed the idea of politics for me. Spending time in Kerala was an attempt to answer the even harder question of *what to do* with that politics, to see if there was some answer beyond the fevered hope of both Right and Left for more material accumulation. If the recovery in the Eastern forest was to sustain itself—if it was to somehow rein-vigorate the human communities I loved, and was to spread to other such places around the world—then economics was as important a subject as government. Much of the eastern United States' natural rejuvenation, for example, came from the assiduous pursuit of the lowest possible food prices, a pursuit that now threatens us with new destruction. The woods recovered when the quest for economic growth and efficiency moved cows from Vermont to Missouri; but the same quest has also just led a South African paper conglomer-ate to buy a huge chunk of Maine, land it could not be expected to manage with any care or affection. Kerala, I sensed, might stand for something different: a place that lived much more self-sufficiently, much closer to home. I hoped that rather than being a backward spot, it might be a forward place, an example not to copy but to keep in mind.

A few weeks of reporting convinced me that Kerala is no para-dise. It has problems: chronic unemployment, for instance, and a stagnant economy that may have enormous trouble coping with world markets. Its budget deficit is often described as out of control. But these are the kinds of problems you find in France. It utterly lacks the squalid drama of the underdeveloped world: the beggars reach-ing through the car window, the children with distended bellies, the baby girls left to die. "I've been all over the Third World for forty years," says Joseph Collins, one of America's leading authorities on hunger. "I was struck by Kerala the whole time I was there. You just don't see malnourished children. You see children with shoes, neatly pressed and washed clothes. People seem to be going to school all the time. It's not like India at all."

A small parade of development experts has passed through Kerala in recent years, mainly to see how its successes might be repeated in Vietnam or Mozambique. But Kerala could be as significant a schoolhouse for the rich world as for the poor. "Kerala is the one large human population on earth which currently meets the sustainability criteria of simultaneous small families and low consumption," says Will Alexander of the Food First Institute in San Francisco.

It is a subversive fact, this little chunk of India, one that could potentially help undermine the developed world's instinctive resistance to change. Kerala's story is not easy to tell—it is an unsexy saga of statistics, of history, of politics in a place too large to be grasped through anecdote. But those statistics are the key to its psychological power for those of us in the West. We may rationally accept that continuing to use the world's resources at our current rate—that living our amazingly high life—is unsustainable. We may, in our rational brains, believe that our car culture, our air-conditioned life, our mall fantasies, are sapping our planet. But in our hearts we fear that any real change would plunge us into a world of poverty, disease, ignorance—that it's either our life in all its detail or a grim, short, narrow life. That's one of the reasons it's been so hard for me to imagine real change in the place where I live; this piece of conventional wisdom has come to seem like political bedrock.

And bedrock in some personal sense as well. I grew up in an American suburb in the 1970s, that is, in the most materially comfortable corner of the most materially comfortable society in the history of the planet. Could I ever cope with living much differently? That's one of the questions that kept nagging at me in Kerala. I spent part of my time there staying in a well-built but spartan dorm at an orphanage and vocational school—Mitraniketan, it was called, "Place of Friends," a kind of secular ashram. Most people in the less-developed world would have loved my small room: it was clean and well built, with water that ran except during frequent blackouts. But there was no washing machine in the dorm: I washed my clothes in the sink. There was no shower; I upended a bucket over my head.

We do not need to emulate such things; there's energy enough, used wisely, to wash our clothes and our hair without wrecking the planet. Still, my small room was a personal reality-check, a reminder that it's one thing to talk about having less, and another thing to *have* less. Is it crazy for me to even consider suggesting a life of less material comfort, of less constant convenience? On the one hand, I am convinced that we need to change many of our habits—maybe eat more of what we grow in our own region, just as a small for instance. But am I too used to convenience and variety to ever change? Am I too used to driving a car everywhere, too used to the freedom from any labor that more money can purchase? After all, I grew up in a suburb. Am I too used to the inefficient privacy of a big house set off by itself?

These, for better and for worse, are the kinds of fundamental questions our environmental crisis raises. If we can't figure out the correct mix of technology and psychology that lets us answer them, then we won't solve the greenhouse effect and the clearcutting and the second-home development and the agribusiness explosion and all the other problems that beset my home place and regions like it around the world. Kerala, unfortunately, offers no answer to the question of our will. But it sharpens the debate, cutting off one line of escape. It gives the lie to the idea that only endless economic growth can produce decent human lives. It's as if someone had shown in a lab that flame didn't require oxygen or that water could freeze at sixty degrees. Suddenly, in the light of Kerala, whole new chemistries of people and society and money and happiness seem at least conceivable.

Kerala supplies no new technology. Its gift is more precious: new fuel for our imaginations. Its example points toward some halfway point where rich and poor might meet and share decent health, where they might provide fine education to their small families, where they might begin to answer that most vexing question, "How much is enough?" It is a clue, not an answer. But an intriguing clue.

★   ★   ★

At the Centre for Development Studies, a Keralite think tank in the capital city of Trivandrum, a historian named P. K. Tharakan has a large stack of books on his desk—each of them, he says, advancing its own thesis about how Kerala had come to be so singular. "Some explain it in terms of social history, some in terms of public policy, maybe public finance." Many Keralites have gone to work in the Persian Gulf and sent their earnings home—that's helped. More important, Kerala elected a communist government in 1957 (the first place on earth to do so in democratic elections) and has since returned the party to power on occasion; clearly that has had much to do with shaping the state, but is it cause or effect? Where did Kerala's feel, its political atmosphere, come from? Some historians point to the type of plantations built by the British, others to benevolent nineteenth-century monarchs. The only thing everyone agrees on is that at least some of the roots of Kerala's peculiarity can be found in its history.

Kerala emerged at the end of the eighth century, as a Hindu monarchy supplanted a looser feudal structure. The trade contacts of the ancient and early medieval periods (Kerala's cardamom, pepper, turmeric, and other spices were constant attractions; and our word "ginger" derives from the local language, Malayalam) eventually turned to more modern, and more exploitative, colonial rule. Vasco da Gama arrived at Calicut in 1498 (the city soon gave its name to calico), followed a century later by the Dutch, with British and French traders on their heels. By 1792 the British were in effective control of what is now Kerala, dividing it into three districts. They governed the northern third, Malabar, directly; Travancore and Cochin to the south retained princely rulers, beholden to the British but with limited administrative freedom—a structure that remained until Independence in 1948 and the decision from New Delhi in 1954 to join the three districts into Kerala.

The first hints of Kerala's singular progress come in the princely states of the south. The rulers there had consolidated power only shortly before the British takeover; according to Tharakan, they needed the backing of the tenant farmers to hold off various local aristocrats. "Development policy in the whole world is generally considered to begin in the 1940s," says Tharakan. "But you can see the roots of it right from the beginning of the nineteenth century in Kerala." The rajahs encouraged agriculture, hoping to build a surplus big enough to satisfy the avarice of both themselves and the British. By giving tax breaks they pushed the reclamation of marshes and swamps, and they moved to give tenants more control over the land.

To conclude that these measures meant Kerala was becoming an enlightened and democratic place, however, would be a mistake. The tradition of caste, bulwark of the Hindu rulers since the eighth century, was as strong as ever in the nineteenth century. At the top of the heap were the Namboodiri Brahmins, followed by the Nairs—soldiers, administrators, farmers and various artisanal classes. Below all of them were the Ezhavas—roughly a fifth of the population, who traditionally made their living climbing coconut trees—and the Pulayas, the local untouchables. Within the various castes innumerable complicated subsets emerged, and the codes of conduct became ever stricter and more degrading over time. Unclean castes had to stay outside the temples: Ezhavas had to stand twelve feet from the walls, and Pulayas sixty-four feet. A Namboodiri walking on the road was preceded by a Nair who gave a warning shout so that others could get out of sight. Low-caste men paid a tax on their hair, and low-caste women paid a breast tax—and the proper salutation from a female to a person of rank was to bare her breast. Umbrellas were forbidden to lower castes (a hardship in this equatorial clime, where much of the population now carries black parasols to ward off the sun). "My grandfather was a Brahmin and could not touch his own children when they got home from school, not until they'd taken a shower," one young woman told me. And the humiliation was accompanied by exploitation. Higher castes, who owned most of the land, could evict the lower castes at will and worked them virtually as slaves. Kumaran Asan, an Ezhava poet, captured the feeling of his people in one verse: "They walk so gently, with fear in mind, that even the earth does not feel their tread . . . even grass would not make way before them."

Kerala is now less caste-ridden than any spot in the Hindu world, a transition more complete than, say, the transformation of the American South achieved by the civil rights movement. Looking backward, it is clear that some of this epic—and mostly peaceful— change can be traced to new economic conditions. For instance, the need for literacy grew as the British and the rajahs pushed cash crops instead of subsistence farming, and as more and more tenant farmers became involved with that market.

But a purely economic explanation of Kerala's singular history goes only so far; it's as unsatisfying as calling the Civil War a clash between industrial and agrarian economies. Such factors loom larger in hindsight; to those who lived through them, the changes seem much more dramatic and less inevitable. "The large masses of people accepted caste distinctions as part of the order of things," writes M. K. Sanoo, a Keralite historian. "Each in his own set place, moving along the orbit of caste, as if it was nature. The men of those days could not even dream that any change in it was possible." Even Tharakan, a devout rationalist, says that "though these changes had an economic base, they were mediated at the level of ethics, of moral dictums." Or in plainer English, Kerala, too, had its Abraham Lincolns, its Martin Luther Kings; and to understand this quick and peaceful miracle—and perhaps to repeat it elsewhere—we need to catch their temper, see the ideas they set loose.

★　　　★　　　★

In proper holy-guy fashion, Sri Narayana Guru was born to an Ezhava family in a hut "but a shade better than a cowshed." His hagiographer relates that Sri Narayana did not cry when he was born: "He lay there without any movement. His father was informed the child was stillborn. Then movement started limb by limb. The father was informed that the child was not dead. Even after that, the cry of the child was not heard. The umbilical cord was cut; still he did not cry. He did not cry even when hungry or for any other reason." As a young man, he renounced worldly attachments and began to wander, sitting with legs crossed in caves and meditating, fasting and consorting with lepers. Even curing lepers, maybe. As more people sought him out for healing or advice, he and his disciples felt the need of a regular temple for worshiping Shiva. At a beautiful spot in a river near Aruvippuram, he had his followers build a small canopy of coconut fronds and mango leaves over an altar on a rock jutting out in the water. "They improvised lamps with shells and arranged them in rows. They were lighted at dusk, and a piper began to play devotional tunes. The whole place was soon filled with pious village folk." Sri Narayana, who had been sitting apart and meditating all night, stood at midnight and walked into the river. As thousands watched silently ("if silence had music, the atmosphere was filled with it," wrote one correspondent) he descended into the river and then reemerged, holding an idol of Shiva. He stood beneath the canopy with the idol in his arms for three hours, totally lost in meditation, tears flowing down his cheeks. Finally, at 3:00 A.M., he installed the idol on the pedestal.

His action was the Keralite equivalent of overturning the tables of the moneychangers, or refusing to give up a seat on the bus. From the beginning of time, so far as anyone knew, only Brahmins had ever installed an idol. "Yet when Swami performed the sacred rite, it appeared so natural for him to pick up a small rock and install it." When Brahmin authorities arrived to question him about his action, he gave an answer that still makes Keralites laugh. "I have installed only the *Ezhava* Shiva," he said, a pious mockery of caste that undermined even more effectively its rotten superstructure.

Caste did not crumble immediately, however; Sri Narayana Guru, along with many other reformers, spent his life in the campaign. Allying himself with a more secular Ezhava reformer, Dr. P. Palpu, Sri Narayana Guru formed a group to fight for increased rights for the Ezhavas: more representation in government jobs, increased educational opportunity, the right to enter and worship at all temples. But all the prosaic struggle for civil rights went on in an atmosphere of spirituality; more than the simple assertion of power by a group too large to be ignored, it was also the assertion of a moral ideal, a view of human dignity against the oppressions both of feudalism and of faith. "One caste, one religion, one God for man," was Narayana Guru's rallying cry, and he clearly meant it—he encouraged any of his followers who wanted more freedom to convert to Christianity ("For your information, I became a Christian before you were born," he once told a visiting priest), explaining his ecumenicism with a simple image: "When the rivers merge in the ocean, is there any difference?"

Since oppression and religion were so intertwined in Hindu culture, social progress depended on religious reform, which could only come from religious leaders—there's a sense in which activists like Sri Narayana Guru had to be both Martin Luther and Martin Luther King. In the rest of India, Gandhi's calls for tolerance seem to have been heeded less than his nationalism; in Kerala, where roadside shrines with busts of Sri Narayana Guru are still garlanded with flowers, the message took firmer root. Sri Narayana Guru had something of the chuckling, inscrutable mystic about him. (My favorite of the reverently collected accounts of his sayings involves an answer he gave to a disciple who asked, "Which is better, burial or cremation?" "Is it not better," answered the swami, "to use the dead body as fertilizer after processing it in a crusher?") But he knew the freedom struggle was about much more than political independence. A student once said that if all the Indians merely spat at the same time, the Englishmen would be drowned. "That is true," said the swami. "But the mouth becomes dry on seeing an Englishman." He was building new people as much as new politics.

Something was in the air—that was clear from the wide range of Keralites who joined the fight against caste and privilege. Groups sprang up within every caste, all with "the avowed goal of exposing superstitions and fighting the inhuman customs and taboos arising from them." To some extent they were shedding old traditions, such as extended families and joint inheritance, that stood in the way of economic modernization. Tharakan calls such changes a "counter-reformation" in response to the lower-caste activism. But there was also a stunning level of class betrayal, of people voluntarily leaving behind old privilege. The story of E. M. S. Namboodiripad, who headed the first communist government in Kerala in 1957, is instructive. Born a Brahmin and a *jenmi*, or rent-collecting landlord, he grew up studying the Rigveda and "scrupulously observing all customs and manners of society handed down from generation to generation." In his autobiography, he recalls his family's extensive lands, "not one square inch cultivated by us." Instead, they sat on the veranda of their estate, giving presents to their serfs and receiving tribute. Awakened by the poetry of Kumaran Asan, who also served as an aide to Narayana Guru, Namboodiripad and others of his clan began to find themselves "gripped by radical ideas and movements." Some burned the sacred threads identifying them as Brahmins and demanded that they be taught English as well as Sanskrit; others argued for reforms of the inheritance traditions of the caste. Namboodiripad inherited a vast fortune in 1940, but he donated it all to start a publishing house for the workers' movement. When he took office in the 1950s, Namboodiripad introduced the land reforms that stripped the last material basis of caste domination.

The moral fervor did not infect all the privileged, many of whom organized to hold on to their position. "From the 1920s on there was a series of constant low-level uprisings," says Franke. "A few deaths here and there, and one very big uprising, the Moplah rebellion." Still, the revolution in people's heads was as thorough as the revolution in material status. "There was such a strong culture of reform," says Franke. "The parallel with the American civil rights movement is a useful one. There came a period here when even closet racists had to at least pay lip service to change. In Nadur, the village I was studying, we lived with a Brahmin family. They were not communists, and they were not *happy* about losing their land, but they did acknowledge that it was morally right." In his book, Franke tells the story of a hot May, when drying wells made fetching water a major task. "A rich high-caste household (whose son is a prominent Marxist) arranged privately for a deep bore to be dug in the rock behind their house." After two days of drilling, they hit water and pumped it with their own diesel motor to a government truck that distributed it daily throughout the village.

The native communism that emerged in Kerala still bears the

KERALA

marks of this intense reform era. As T. M. Thomas Isaac, a professor at the Centre for Development Studies, writes in a history of industrial workers in Kerala, the legacy of Sri Narayana Guru and his contemporaries was a sense of pride and self-respect among lower-caste laborers. Having entered politics through the fights to open temples or other such campaigns, many went from from caste militance to class consciousness. For them, "One caste, one religion, one God for man" was replaced as a slogan by "No caste, no religion, no God for man," and they thought of themselves as workers, not Ezhavas. But when elected to office, the Keralite communists managed to avoid the lunacies that characterized Marxist governments elsewhere. For all the struggle, there was enough flexibility, enough *morality*, so that the search for justice never turned into social cleansing.

For those of us who live in the rich parts of the world, the most moving part of the story is probably the painful decision of the well-off to trade in their old privilege for something fairer. Those who did so were rarely saints; in some ways, the most moving story I heard involves at least as much calculation as nobility. P. K. Nambiar, a retired veterinarian who guided me on a visit to Trivandrum, described his upbringing in a well-off Nair-caste family. They owned two thousand acres—a vast holding in Kerala, where the average spread today is an acre or two—all of which was farmed by tenants. "I can remember, even now, the depressed classes would come to my father's house. They'd have to stay three hundred meters away. They'd bring a live fish as a tribute and dig a little hole in the ground so the fish would not move away, and then they'd make a little sound so we'd know the fish was there." When he went away to school, his mother would make him take a bath when he came home on break before she'd touch him—"she'd insist right now that you wash your

133

," he said, as we finished our tea. "But my father somehow knew that land reform would eventually come, and he decided to give away his land himself. The taxes on it were high anyway. And as a result, all of our tenants, even today, are very cordial with us—not like they are with those who held out to the bitter end. When my mother died recently, we returned to our old lands to cremate her. And I was a little worried about what people there would say. But they were wonderful. It is customary that the nearest tenant provide the logs for the pyre, and he was grateful to do so."

★   ★   ★

In the morning every road in Kerala is lined with boys and girls walking to school. Their uniforms are bright blue, bright green, bright red, depending on the school; it may be sentimental to say that their eyes are bright as well, but of all the subtle corrosives that broke down the old order and gave rise to the new Kerala, surely none is as important as the spread of education to an extent unprecedented and as yet unmatched in the Third World. Education has been both cause and effect of Kerala's development, breeding new demands for progress and offering the example of other parts of the world. (It has also kept Keralite labor in demand around the globe—as many as a quarter million of the state's residents work in the Persian Gulf at any moment, sending most of their wages home.) "One day I was talking with an eleven-year-old from a poor fishing family," said Joseph Collins, the development expert. "He said, 'Maybe I'll see you in the United States someday—that's probably where I'll go for my doctorate.'"

Though Christian missionaries and the British started the process, it took the militance of the caste-reform groups and then of the budding Left to spread education widely; the first great boom was in the 1920s and 1930s—particularly in southern Kerala, where the princes acceded to popular demands for ever more schools. When leftists dominated politics in the 1960s, they spread the educational programs into Malabar, the northern state that had been ruled directly by the British, and began granting scholarships to untouchables and tribal peoples. By 1981 the general literacy rate in Kerala was 70 percent—twice the all-India rate of 36 percent. Even more impressively, the rural literacy rate was just as high, and female literacy—at 66 percent—not far behind. Kerala was a bizarre spike on the dismal chart of Third World literacy.

The government, particularly the leftists who governed for much of the late 1980s, continued to press the issue, however, aiming for "total literacy," defined by the United Nations as a population in which about 95 percent can read and write. The pilot project began in the Ernakulam region, an area of 3 million people that includes the city of Cochin. In late 1988 fifty thousand volunteers fanned out around the district, tracking down 175,000 illiterates between the ages of five and sixty, two-thirds of whom were women. The leftist Peoples Science Movement (KSSP) recruited twenty thousand volunteer tutors and sent them out to teach: it was hoped that within a year the illiterates would read Malayalam at thirty words a minute, copy a text at seven words a minute, count and write from one to a hundred, and add and subtract three-digit numbers. The larger goal was to make people feel powerful, feel involved—the early lessons were organized around Brazilian teacher Paolo Freire's notion that the concrete problems of people's lives provide the best teaching material. KSSP organizers might appear in a village, drumming and dancing; as a crowd

gathered, perhaps one of the teachers would start to sing, adapting
a Bertolt Brecht poem:

> Do not hesitate
> The old and the young
> Worker and farmer
> Begin studying today
> To read and write . . .
> Study everything
> Question everything
> Do not hesitate
> Take a book in hand
> It is the new weapon

"Classes were held in cowsheds, in the open air, in courtyards,"
one leader told the *New York Times*. "For fishermen we went to the
seashore. In the hills, tribal groups sat on rocks. Leprosy patients
were taught to hold a pencil in stumps of hands with rubber bands.
We have not left anyone out." For those with poor eyesight, volunteers
collected seventy-five thousand donated pairs of old eyeglasses and
learned from optometrists how to match them with recipients. On
February 4, 1990, thirteen months after the initial canvass, Indian
Prime Minister V. P. Singh marked the start of World Literacy
Year with a trip to Ernakulam, declaring it the country's first totally
literate district. Of the 175,000 students, 135,000 scored 80 percent
or better on the final test, putting the region's official literacy rate
above 96 percent; many of the others stayed in follow-up classes and
likely had learned enough to read bus signs. The total cost of the 150
hours of education was about twenty-six dollars per person.

In the course of the lessons, writes Franke, teachers also tried to teach some basic civics, as well as messages on how to deal with the government, hygiene, "the dignity of work, equality of the sexes, the need for clean drinking water, how to read a clock, and what immunizations should be given to one's children at what ages." (Partly because of those lessons, Kerala recently reported 100 percent childhood immunization rates for tuberculosis, diptheria, polio, whooping cough, and tetanus). Tharakan, who studied some of the literacy programs, reports traveling to a village where he met twelve older people thought to be illiterate. "I wanted to find out what they knew of the world, so I asked them questions like 'What is the capital of Zimbabwe?' and 'Who is the president of Angola?' All twelve of them knew." (An American university professor and I were interviewing Tharakan and nodded sagely at this anecdote. In the hall outside we turned to each other and said, as one, "What *is* the capital of Zimbabwe?") Journalists have traditional measures of their own for gauging these things—one day, I was surrounded by small children at a Hindu temple school who wanted to ask a million questions about America, so I tested them with the name of the president. "Billclinton, Billclinton," they shrieked; later I met a small boy who got the answer wrong, insisting it was Algore. "The average Keralite agricultural laborer will know more about international affairs than the average American," says Thomas Isaac, the Marxist professor at the Centre for Development Studies. "I am not joking."

But what really matters is not mere knowledge. Organizers knew the literacy campaign was working when letters from the newly literate began arriving in government offices, demanding paved roads or hospitals. As one analysis of the program concludes: "Those who have felt the power of learning know they have rights.

They are willing to struggle for them. Such people constitute a democratic force [to] which even a government ostensibly committed to their welfare must pay attention or face direction." In other words, the government had created citizens able to hold it accountable. They are no longer marginal humans.

★   ★   ★

West across the Ghat mountains, in the neighboring state of Tamil Nadu, a new industry has sprung up in recent years. Quack doctors claim to be able to tell, from the appearance of a newborn's umbilical cord, whether the *next* child will be a boy or a girl. If they say it's a she, the mother often opts for an abortion (a twig of the poisonous erukkam plant is inserted into her cervix) as soon as she gets pregnant; should the procedure not work, the flowers of the plant yield a milk that can kill newborn females. When two *Washington Post* reporters began looking into the issue in 1993, they traveled to Madras, in Tamil Nadu, where they came across a recent survey by the Community Service Guild—it concluded that of the 1,250 women surveyed, more than half had killed baby daughters. One woman who had poisoned her newborn daughter told the reporters, "I never felt any sorrow. There was a lot of bitterness in my heart toward the baby because the gods should have given me a son." The cities may be higher-tech—amniocentesis is now widespread in urban India—but are otherwise much the same. Of eight thousand abortions performed at one Bombay clinic after parents knew the sex of the child, 7,999 were of female fetuses. Even those girl children allowed to live are often given less food, less education, and less health care—a bias not confined to India. Elizabeth Bumiller titled her book on Indian women, *May You Be the Mother of a Hundred Sons*, after a traditonal Hindu wedding blessing; but in Muslim Pakistan there are only ninety-two women for every hundred men, and boys are twice as likely to be taken to the hospital as girls are. In Africa the *Post* reporters found clinics where only boys were lined up for treatment. In times of famine, the director said, daughters were simply left to die. "No one will even take them to a clinic. They prefer the boy to survive." In China, with its fierce birth control, there were 113 boys for every 100 girls under the age of one in 1990—even though, all things being equal, women naturally outnumber men. There are, in short, millions and millions of women missing around the world—women who would be there were it not for the dictates of custom and economy.

So it is a remarkable achievement in Kerala to say simply this: there are more women than men. In India as a whole there are about 929 women per 1,000 men; in Kerala the number is 1,040 women, about where it should be. The female life expectancy in Kerala exceeds the male, just as it does in the developed world. Infant mortality is actually lower for girls than for boys. There are actually more female than male college students.

As with education, the emancipation of women is both cause and effect of Kerala's singular progress. To some extent, it has historical roots: by ancient custom the Nair caste of Hindus, who made up about 15 percent of the population, lived in joint households. Much studied by anthropologists, these *taravads* owned all household property in common. A husband could marry into the *taravad*, but doing so won him no permanent rights to property—or even to his wife. In some communities, when the man returned from a journey (the Nairs were, after all, a warrior caste), he had to wait on a special bench on the porch of the house for his wife to invite him in; if his sandals were out on the veranda, it was the sign that she had taken a new husband. Women took lovers for the night— a man's sword warned others that he was there, much like the sock on the doorknob in a college dorm. This female control over sexuality and property began to fade when the British took over. Without wars to fight, the men stayed home and became increasingly interested in knowing who their children were; later the complex joint holdings made modern capitalism cumbersome, and what remained of them were largely broken up by land reforms. Still, some of the ancient attitude remains. Keralite women brim with a confidence that would shock their sisters in the rest of India—and most of the rest of the developing world. I spent several days at the secular ashram—Mitraniketan, thirty miles from Trivandrum—sharing a dormitory with about twenty-five women from villages around Kerala who had gathered there for "awareness training." They were like a bright, moving cloud in their saris; many were midwives or other health workers, and they would return home to spread the word about everything from managing finances to breast-feeding. Though many were married, they felt free to travel on their own. (A solitary Muslim husband had come along to chaperone his wife and her sister.) And on the last night of the program, in a packed auditorium, they performed more than an hour's worth of skits and songs, taking the stage one after another without any shyness or giggling modesty. One long song, which kept the audience rapt, involved a girl who had married the man of her dreams, only to see him start drinking. He repents, but then he drinks again. Finally, he hits her. And she packs up and leaves. Amid much cheering. Loretta Lynn would feel right at home.

Just as Kerala has managed to free itself from the caste discrimination endemic on the subcontinent, and much of the misogyny that rules the Third World, it has also won the war against communal hatred that has helped make progress in the rest of India so difficult. Despite a longstanding commitment by the national government to secularism, communal strife has roiled the subcontinent for the last fifty years, rising and falling in intensity. The most recent clashes began in 1991, when an avowedly Hindu political party, the BJP, managed to become the largest opposition bloc in the Indian parliament. Its nakedly fundamentalist appeal was symbolized by its denunciation of a particular mosque that had been built five hundred years earlier on a hill in the North Indian town of Ayodhya, where certain devout Hindus believe the god Ram was born. After its election successes the BJP called for a march on Ayodhya, which quickly got out of hand: Hindu militants demolished the mosque, setting off the inevitable reaction from Muslims across India, setting off in turn a bloody counterreaction from Hindus, which turned especially murderous in Bombay.

In Kerala, too, there was trouble—isolated rioting and even deaths. But religious diversity in Kerala dates back to the first century, when Saint Thomas founded seven churches. When the Muslims arrived six centuries later, they also used conversion and not conquest to win souls. Tolerance is deeply ingrained; within days of the trouble at Ayodhya, several million common people signed petitions carried from village to village, stating their opposition to violence.

The BJP targeted Kerala as a potential source of recruits but in the 1987 elections, though it was surging nationally, won none of the 122 seats it contested in the state assembly. As the country's poverty has worsened, says Thomas Isaac, "there are plenty of people who would like the Muslims to be the problem, just like the Jews in Germany." But his just-completed analysis of the 1992 elections shows that while the BJP's vote totals exceeded 40 percent in other parts of the country, in Kerala they had dropped to about 5 percent.

★   ★   ★

Whatever the historical reasons, Kerala's quartet of emancipations—from caste distinction, religious hatred, the worst forms of gender discrimination, and the powerlessness of illiteracy—have left the state with a distinctive feel, a flavor of place that influences every aspect of its life. It is, for one thing, an intensely political region: early in the morning in tea shops across Kerala people eat a *dosha* and read one of the two or three Malayalam-language papers that arrive on the first bus. (Kerala has the highest newspaper consumption per capita of any spot in India.) In each town square political parties maintain their icons: a statue of Indira Gandhi (the white streak in her hair carefully painted in) or a portrait of Marx, Engels, and Lenin in careful profile. (Kerala may be the last spot on earth where socialist realism is not camp.) Strikes, agitations, and "stirs"—a sort of wildcat job action—are so common as to be almost unnoticeable. One morning's edition of the *Indian Express* covered a bus strike, a planned strike of medical students over "unreasonable exam schedules," and the call from one leftist leader that the government take over a coat factory where striking workers had been locked out. By the next day's paper the bus strike had ended, but a bank strike had begun. Worse, the men who perform the traditional and much beloved *Kathakali* dance—a stylized ballet that can last all night—were threatening to strike and planning a march in full costume and makeup through the streets of the capital.

Sometimes all the disputation can get overwhelming. In a long account of his home village, Thulavady, K. E. Verghese says, "Politics are much in the air and it is difficult to escape from them. Even elderly women who are not interested are dragged into politics." After several fights, he reports, a barbershop posted a sign on the wall: "No political discussions please." But for the most part the various campaigns and protests seem a sign of self-confidence and political vitality, a vast improvement over the apathy, powerlessness, ignorance, or tribalism that governs too many Third World communities. Franke describes recent history in the town he studied, Nadur, where in 1981 a local communist leader began an effort to agitate for a new electrical transformer. (Only a quarter of the households have electricity, but everyone benefits from streetlights.) With the old transformer, the current—though rated at 220 volts—was so weak that in the early evening the streetlights hardly glowed. As the few people with private lamps began to turn them off around 10:00 P.M., and the current began to strengthen, the streetlights flared to life long after they were of any use. A petition drive and some demonstrations at regional offices finally got a new substation built. A year later the same villagers forced the paving of the main road, which was nearly impassable during the rainy season and a dusty mess the rest of the year. "Whenever buses or taxis came along, the dust would be everywhere. It would even go into people's houses." The protest was fierce but nonviolent, and the road was paved—dust no longer washed into people's homes, which is a major political victory if dust has always coated your dinner.

Elsewhere in India, personality cults dominate political life. (In neighboring Tamil Nadu, the longtime chief minister is a woman whose picture is, literally, everywhere. Giant cardboard cutouts of her, some of them forty feet high, tower above intersections. When I was there recently, Keralites were snickering at the news that one of the cutouts had fallen over, destroying four cars.) But Keralites are far more self-assured. "You can go to any village in Kerala, and no one will tremble before you because you are a white person," Thomas Isaac told me, and he was correct. For those used to the all-too-explicable servility of poor people in other parts of the world (and to the occasional, and equally explicable, rage that such obsequiousness can suddenly turn to), Kerala offers a refreshing whiff of the air that George Orwell found in revolutionary Spain in the 1930s. "Waiters and shop-walkers looked you in the face and treated you as an equal. Servile and even ceremonial forms of speech had disappeared. . . . All this was queer and moving." Once when leaving for India, I was trapped by a snowstorm and spent two days in Manhattan, seeing the usual winter sight of beggars huddled in blankets against the cold with pitiful signs scrawled in cardboard at their feet. Finally landing in Bombay, I took a taxi from the international airport to the domestic terminal, and in the ten-minute journey four separate women with clinging children reached through the window asking for alms. (Not surprising, since a million people live in cardboard huts lining the airport runways; it is one of the world's largest slums.) To reach Kerala, which of course is much poorer than New York, and in fact trails Bombay in per capita income, was a relief—queer and moving indeed.

★　　　★　　　★

The communists have come and gone from power several times since Independence; in the early 1990s they were out of power, and even when they've been in control it's usually been as part of a coalition. But the political culture of Kerala—the egalitarianism, the willingness to agitate—has bred a particular strain of thinking that seems to last even through conservative administrations. "There is a Left ideological hegemony," says Thomas Isaac; translated from the Marxist, the watchword of Keralite politics has been "redistribution." Where other poor places—Japan after the war, Taiwan, South Korea, Brazil, the new Mexico—focused on growth to alleviate poverty, Kerala has been much more interested in sharing what wealth is available. And the most obvious goal of the various revolutionaries, as it has been in almost every agrarian economy, was land reform—sharing the very soil. K. E. Verghese, in his chronicle of the village of Thulavady, describes the old rural economy as "semi-slavery." The landlords, the *jenmis*, were often exempt from taxes while the tenants had to pay rent or face eviction. The sharecroppers were paying the landlords between 60 and 80 percent of the *gross* returns; as late as the 1960s, 8 percent of landowning households controlled better than 60 percent of rice land. Such feudalism, of course, is typical across Asia and Latin America.

When the communist government took power in Kerala's first election in 1957, it seemed as if decades of struggle, principally by the Kerala Farmers Association, would be immediately rewarded. But landlords organized to fight, appealing to the central government. Three weeks after the major land-reform law was passed, the Congress government in Delhi dismissed the communists and introduced presidential rule. India's high court declared the law unconstitutional. But the agitation continued; in some places tenants stopped waiting for reform and ceased paying rent on their own. Often they planted red flags in their fields. And in the late 1960s they returned to power the communists, who this time managed to pass a law that stood up in court. About 1.5 million tenants became landowners, with about one and half acres of rice land apiece. More than a third of a million of the poorest Keralites received the rights to the hut land they had been living on, gaining compounds large enough to grow a few coconut trees.

Although the land reform redistributed acreage, it didn't completely even out the distribution of wealth. Time after time I talked with the descendants of Brahmin families who had used the compensation from the taking of their land to get good educations, land professional jobs, and maintain relatively high incomes. But, as Franke points out, these doctors, teachers, and civil servants do some good for Kerala, instead of earning their wealth by collecting rent in the fashion of their ancestors. The huge slice of profit they took off the top of each year's crop has been effectively redistributed. And undoubtedly the relative moderation of Kerala's land reform has been one of its blessings. Landowners were compensated for their property, and the communists made no attempts to collectivize agriculture, content to let the new owners farm it as they saw fit.

I am, of course, aware that speaking about communism, even the tame form found in Kerala, is no more popular in the aftermath of the Soviet collapse than discussing snowstorms in April. Who wants to hear about it? When Newt Gingrich calls Bill Clinton a "McGovernnik" for proposing health care reform, who wants to even mention the word? And yet I suspect that once the current triumphalism ceases, the beneficiaries of the end of Bolshevism may include those economists and union organizers and priests of the sensible Left who will be free to talk about equity and redistribution—without having to defend the labor camps and secret police and belching heavy industry and all the other major and minor horrors of Leninism. My home place, and indeed the rest of the world, have no need of Kerala's Marxist trappings; but we may have much to learn from its commitment to fairness.

If there's a general lesson about socialism provided by Kerala, it's that the government benefits from having to answer to voters. The Keralite communists have ruled a population bigger than Czechoslovakia, East Germany, Hungary, Cuba, or North Vietnam; they have accomplished all of the things those nations insisted they were also accomplishing; and they have done so without closing newspapers, jailing opponents, or utterly destroying the environment. Most of all, perhaps, they have helped produce a population of people able to hold them, and all other would-be leaders, accountable—able to demand for themselves the goods that Soviet leaders dispensed as favors.

Chief among those goods is food. The fight for fairly priced food was part of the general upheaval of the years before Independence: militants staged antihoarding campaigns and forced landlords to sell surpluses at affordable rates. The first communist government tried to institutionalize some of these measures; but after Delhi dissolved it, efforts languished until 1964, when a famine forced the state to buy food to ensure its availability. The system of ration or "fair-price" shops that was set up then, in collaboration with the CARE relief agency, quickly spread—99 percent of the state's villages are served by one of the stores, which offer rice at a steep discount. Each family gets a ration of the cheap rice, depending on how much paddy land it owns. When Franke studied the village of Nadur, he found that the poorer residents bought two-thirds of their rice at the store—and a much higher percentage during the lean months of the summer—thereby effectively raising the incomes of the poorest fifth of the population by 10 percent.

There is no question that food is often scarce. In Nadur, says Franke, during the hot and dry months of February and March, "food is mango stew, mango curry, mango pickle, fried mango, mango snacks, and mango dessert." But malnutritional diseases like kwashiorkor have virtually disappeared, partly because what calories do exist are shared much more equitably than in most places. Just as important—and a fact that underlines both Kerala's poverty and its uniqueness—the calories that do get eaten get put to use. In a body infested with intestinal parasites, as much as half the food that goes in the mouth nourishes only the worms. Because Kerala offers affordable medical care at clinics spread across the state, there are fewer worms. This is what much of the world is about—are the worms in your gut eating half of your food?

★   ★   ★

Many people sincerely alarmed by the world's ever expanding population have decided that we need laws to stop the growth—that sad as such coercion would be, it's a necessary step. And they have some cases to point—to China, for instance, where massive government force probably did manage to contain a population that would otherwise have grown beyond its ability to feed itself. But as that country frees itself from the grip of the communists, the pent-up demand for children may well touch off a massive baby boom. "Compulsion *does not work* in birth control," writes Paul Harrison in his book *The Third Revolution*; and his case in point is India, which tried to raise its rate of sterilization dramatically in the 1970s. To obtain recruits for the "vasectomy camps" erected throughout the country, the government withheld licenses for shops and vehicles, refused to grant food ration cards or to supply canal water for irrigation, and in some cases simply sent the police to round up "volunteers." It worked, in a sense: in 1976, 8.3 million Indians were sterilized. But Indira Gandhi lost the next election as a result, the campaign was called off, and it was "ten years before modern contraception rose again to its 1972–73 peak." India's population, which grew by 109 million in the 1960s and by 137 million in the 1970s, grew by 160 million in the 1980s. That is the population of two Mexicos, or one 1965 United States.

The population problem seems so overwhelming that we're always looking for shortcuts. In dark moments it's been said that diseases like AIDS might be the start of the earth trying to reduce its overpopulation. Morality aside, the idea is simply wrong, for it underestimates the sheer momentum of the increase. (Half a million Rwandans were hacked to death in that country's brief civil war; it took the world about forty-seven hours to replace them.) And by killing those in their prime, writes Harrison, war and disease simply deepen chaos and divert resources from health and education, making life less predictable and delaying the shift to lower fertility that comes with stability. As usual, immorality is bad policy.

In any event, Kerala—and a scattered collection of other places around the world that are now drawing new attention in the wake of the UN's Cairo summit on population—makes clear that neither plague nor coercion is necessary. In Kerala the birth rate is now eighteen per thousand; nearly the same as America's, 40 percent below India as a whole, and almost 60 percent below the rate for poor countries in general. "Some districts will reach zero population growth before the United States," one expert told me. Thus, Kerala has solved one-third of the equation that drives environmental destruction the world over. And, defying the conventional wisdom, it has done so without rapid economic growth—done so without becoming a huge consumer of resources and thereby destroying the environment in other ways.

I sat one afternoon in the office of M. N. Sivaram—the Trivandrum representative of the International Family Planning Association—a spare room lined with birth control posters. "The two-child family is the social norm here now," he said. "Even among illiterate women we find it's true. When we send our surveyors out, people are embarrassed to say if they have more than two kids. Seven or eight years ago the norm was three children, and we thought we were doing pretty good. Now it's two, and among the most educated people it's one." Many factors contribute to the new notion of what's proper: the pressure on land is intense, and most people can't support huge families on their small parcels. But that hasn't stopped others elsewhere in the world. More powerful, perhaps, is the spread of education across Kerala. Literate women are better able to take charge of their lives—the typical woman marries at twenty-two in Kerala, compared with eighteen in the rest of India. Worldwide, literate women average two children less than uneducated women. They also want a good education for their children. In many cases that means private schools to supplement the public education, and most people can't afford several tuitions.

Kerala's remarkable access to affordable health care has provided a similar double blessing. There's a clinic every few kilometers where

IUDs are inserted for free—that helps. But the same clinic provides free health care for children, and that helps even more. With virtually all mothers taught to breast-feed, and a state-supported nutrition program for pregnant and new mothers, infant mortality in 1991 was seventeen per thousand, compared with ninety-one for low-income countries generally. Someplace between those two figures—seventeen and ninety-one—lies the point where people become confident their children will survive. The typical fertility rate for traditional societies, says Harrison, is about seven children per woman, which "represents not just indiscriminate breeding, but the result of careful strategy." Women needed one or two sons to take care of them if they were widowed; and where child mortality was high, this meant having three sons and, on average, six children." In a society where girls seem as useful as boys, and where children die infrequently, reason suddenly dictates one or two kids. "I have one child, and I am depending on her to survive," said Mr. Sivaram. "If I ever became insecure about that, perhaps my views would change."

Sivaram said something else that interested me. He was puffing a cigarette as we talked. "I know smoking is dangerous," he said. "But I'm not fully *aware* it's dangerous. Or else I would stop. Everyone in Kerala is fully aware about family planning." Smoking, oddly, is one of the few areas where we in the West *have* changed. Despite the best efforts of the tobacco lobby, we've reached an *awareness* about the stupidity of cigarette smoking, an awareness reflected in the declining smoking rate. Along with increased recycling, it's one of the few positive trends we can point to in our country. Such awareness —some new level of understanding where self-interest and public interest intersect to leave behind a new attitude and a changed behavior—is clearly essential about such issues as mass transit and conservation and living lightly. The Keralite experience indicates such awareness comes through widespread, self-reinforcing change. People have fewer children in this pocket of India because life is safer, fairer, more decent. Because they have fewer children, life should be safer, fairer, more decent in the future.

*   *   *

The question *should* be: how can the Kerala model spread to other places with different cultures, less benign histories? Unfortunately, there's another question about the future that needs to be answered first. Can the Kerala model survive even in Kerala, or will it be remembered chiefly as an isolated and short-term outbreak from a prison of poverty?

In the paddy fields near Mitraniketan, bare-chested men swung hoes hard into the newly harvested fields, preparing the ground for the next crop. They worked steadily but without hurry, in part because there was no next job to get to. Unemployment and underemployment have been signal problems in Kerala for decades. As much as a quarter of the state's population may be without jobs; in rural villages, by many estimates, laborers are happy for seventy or eighty days a year of hoe-and-sickle work. And though the liberal pension and unemployment compensation laws, as well as the land reform that has left most people with at least a few coconut trees in their house compound, buffer the worst effects of joblessness, it is nonetheless a real problem: in mid-morning in the small village at the edge of the rice fields, young men lounge in doorways with nothing to do.

To some extent, Kerala's successes are surely to blame. A recent report published by the Centre for Development Studies looked at the coir (coconut fiber), cashew processing, and cigarette industries and concluded that as unions succeeded in raising wages and improving working conditions, they were also driving factories off to more degraded parts of India. Kerala's vaunted educational system may also play a role. Because of what they are taught, writes M.A. Oommen, "university graduates become seekers of jobs rather than creators of jobs." In Kerala, says K. K. George of the Centre for Development Studies, "the concept of a job is a job in a ministry. When you get out of school you think, 'The state should give me a job as a clerk' "—an understandable attitude, since government service is relatively lucrative, completely secure, and over by law at age fifty-five. Large numbers of Keralites also go into medicine, law, education; that they perform well is proved by their success in finding jobs abroad, but at home there is less demand.

The combination of a stagnant economy and a strong commitment to providing health and education have left the state facing large budget deficits. Development expert Joseph Collins, for all his praise of Kerala's progress, calls it a "bloated social welfare state without the economy to support it," a place that has developed a "populist welfare culture, where all the parties are into promising more goodies, which means more deficits. The mentality that things don't have to be funded, that's strong in Kerala—in the midst of the fiscal crisis that was going on while I was there, some of the parties were demanding that the agricultural pension be doubled."

But the Left seems to be waking up to the problems. Professor Thomas Isaac—whom one colleague called a "twenty-four-karat Marxist" and who serves on the central committee of the communist party—says "our main effort has been to redistribute, not to manage the economy. But because we on the Left have real power, we need to have an active interest in that management to formulate a new policy toward production." Instead of building huge factories or lowering wages to grab jobs from elsewhere or collectivizing farmers, the Left has embarked on a series of "new democratic initiatives" that come as close as anything on the planet to actually incarnating "sustainable development," that buzzword most beloved of environmentalists. The Left has proposed, and on a small scale begun, the "People's Resource Mapping Program," an attempt to move beyond word literacy to "land literacy." Residents of local villages have begun assembling detailed maps of their area, showing topography, soil type, depth to the water table, and depth to bedrock. Information in hand, local people could sit down and see where a grove of trees would make sense to prevent erosion. And the mapmakers think about local human problems, too. In one village, residents were spending scarce cash during the dry season to buy vegetables imported from elsewhere in India. Paddy owners were asked to lease their land free of charge between rice crops for big market gardens, which were sited by referring to the maps of the water table. More than two thousand unemployed youths were paid to tend the gardens, and the vegetables were sold at the local market for less than the cost of the imports. This is not central planning, but neither is it the global market in action. It is exquisitely local; it demands democracy, literacy, participation, cooperation. The new vegetables represent "economic growth" of a sort that does much good and no harm. The number of dollars—and, hence, the liters of oil consumed—go down, not up. It is something my Adirondack neighbors and I could figure out a hundred ways to emulate, if we could first overcome the devotion to separateness that rules our economic lives.

With Kerala's high level of education and ingrained commitment to fairness, such novel strategies might well solve its economic woes—especially since a stabilized population means it doesn't need to sprint simply to stay in place. One can easily imagine a state that manages to put more of its people to work for livable, if low, wages. They would manufacture items that they need to use, grow their own food, and participate in the world economy in a modest way: exporting workers and some high-value foods like spices, and attracting some tourists. I spent several days at an orphanage and training school outside Trivandrum run by a Gandhian disciple, Vishwanathan. He cut a splendid figure in his full beard and his outfit of locally made white khadi cloth; and as we wandered the grounds of his secular ashram, he would talk about Kerala's future. "Instead of urbanization, ruralization," he says. "Small satellite industries." At his cooperative, farmers learn to grow silkworms and women learn to repair small motors, solder together broken transistor radios—to make things last, to build a small-scale economy of permanence that our grandparents might recognize but is light years away from our present day. "We don't need to become commercial agents, to always be buying and selling this and that," says Vishwanathan. He talks on into the evening, spinning a future both humble and exceedingly pleasant, much like the tree-shaded and airy community he has built on once-abandoned land. A future as close to the one envisioned by E. F. Schumacher or Thomas Jefferson or Gandhi as is currently imaginable on this planet. "What is the good life?" asks Vishwanathan. "The good life is to be a good neighbor; to consider your neighbor as yourself."

★　　　★　　　★

Ah, neighbors. In a global economy, pretty much everyone is your neighbor; and with the introduction of GATT and the opening of India's economy, these neighbors may soon overwhelm Kerala's history, its leftist tradition, its demographic success. Neighbors are pressing in so fast that we may never know if Kerala, left to its own devices, could solve its problems.

"India," the regional director for Coca-Cola said recently, "is the last major market on earth." Walled off since Independence from much of the world's economy by laws and tariffs, India has been a multinational bit player—thirty-third among exporting nations, trailing Ireland. Its economy has been growing "only" 4 percent a year, nothing like the double-digit rates in China, which is now held up as the model of a booming nation. As the *New York Times* news story put it, rather baldly: "Where the single-minded determination and decisiveness of an authoritarian leader pushed China rapidly into the world economy, India's torturous and corrupt democratic politics, coupled with a lingering nostalgia for socialism, and a pervasive xenophobia, have hobbled real economic development." But not to fear: in the past four years India has begun to jog down the Chinese track, promising the International Monetary Fund that in return for loans, it will "structurally adjust" itself, a form of economic chiropractic that has been prescribed for poor countries from Albania to Zaire. In real terms, it means bringing down budget deficits, usually by slashing social spending; eliminating subsidies, sometimes even for basic foodstuffs; and beginning to open one's sheltered economy to the bracing air of the outside world.

In even more real terms, what it means to Keralites can be measured in the price of coconuts. "When you look around Kerala, you see nothing but coconut trees," says Thomas Isaac. "When you fly in on a plane, you see all the coconut trees and wonder where you might possibly land." Kerala *means* "land of coconuts." By Franke's calculation, three coconut trees can supply enough money to buy food for one adult for a year, as long as coconuts are selling at four rupees apiece. But with the arrival of "liberalization" and the lifting of tariffs, says Thomas Isaac, the price of coconuts has plummeted 50 percent. Meanwhile, the state subsidy for foods like rice has also dropped precipitously, to the point where Kerala has been forced to close the fair-price ration shops to many who used to depend on them; subsidized rice purchases dropped by nearly a tenth from 1992 to 1993. "All this may turn out to be an insurmountable obstacle to our system," says Thomas Isaac. "Rightly or wrongly, we've been pursuing a path of development autonomous from the outside world. We don't have so much faith in integration with the outside world on its terms, you know—you have to remember we were integrated for several hundred years under colonialism. But now we are forced to integrate, and whatever local interventions we try to make in Kerala may come to naught against this force."

Though there will be resistance—India's "torturous democracy" guarantees that closing factories and raising prices will take longer than in the marvelously efficient China—the handwriting seems to be on the wall, just as it is in this hemisphere with the signing of NAFTA, and around the world with the passage of GATT. "It is given to us—we can't rebel," says Tharakan, the economic historian. It is a force of history every bit as powerful as, say, British colonialism, or the wave of independence movements sparked by the Indian example. "The logic in Kerala has been the logic of the village," says Thomas Isaac. "The logic of the national reform is private."

Structural adjustment, often accompanied by forced loan

repayment, has a mixed record at best; most Latin American and African countries have cut spending on health and education drastically in the 1980s, slipping further back into poverty. And opening to the outside world has generally increased inequality. One study found that in the "most penetrated" economies, even if the total GNP was growing like a weed, the average person ate 730 fewer calories a day and 21 less grams of protein than did a person in a more protected economy. Still, it is easy enough to see why sincere people, not just Coca-Cola salespeople, might favor such a strategy for India. Across the nation, nearly half a billion people live in absolute poverty, fewer than 10 percent have adequate sanitation, nearly 15 percent of children die before the age of five, half the people can't read, communal violence festers amid the ignorance. For all its democratic traditions, its ancient heritage, and its huge middle class, India is a disaster. If you didn't know the story of Kerala—that a sweeping commitment to equity and redistribution works social wonders even without growing the economy—you might conclude there was no other path for India to truly develop besides all-out Western-style economic growth.

But there is a bigger question lurking here. Suppose for a moment Kerala could adapt to the modern outside world—given its high level of education, that is at least a possibility. Say it becomes a new Thailand or Taiwan, and say—just for the sake of argument—that India emerges as the next Asian tiger, with an economy booming as vibrantly as China's. Suppose that in a decade the *Times* could write as glowingly of India as it did of China—"Everything from McDonnell Douglas passenger jets to desktop computers, buckets of Kentucky Fried Chicken to McDonald's hamburgers are made in China. More than 15,000 Avon representatives troop door to door in Guangzhou; chuppies, China's young entrepreneurs, stick pocket-sized cellular phones in their ears with . . . panache." Suppose, even, that the new wealth was shared somewhat equitably: not like in China, where the rural peasantry is languishing jealously; not like in Brazil, where famine grew in the very shadow of the economic miracle. Suppose all these things happened. Even then, it would be a tragedy of sorts—a waste of the lesson that is Kerala.

Because Kerala suggests a way out of two problems simultaneously: not only the classic development goal of more calories in bellies and more shoes on feet, but also the emerging, equally essential, task of living *lightly* on the earth, using fewer resources, creating less waste. Kerala's environmental importance is utterly basic. Kerala demonstrates that a low-level economy can create a decent life, abundant in the things—health, education, community—that are most necessary for us all. Remember, Kerala's per capita GNP in 1986 was $330, while the U.S. GNP was $17,480. And GNP is an eloquent shorthand for gallons of gasoline burned, stacks of garbage tossed out, quantities of timber sawn into boards. Every dollar spent, remember, means burning half a liter of oil.

For years development experts have debated which is more important: growth or redistribution. The answer is that either can work for *development*. That is, Japan rebuilt itself, mostly by growing its economy, into the most prosperous place on the planet, while Kerala shared its way to a set of demographic statistics quite close to the Japanese level. It is also true that a country can follow either strategy and still not develop. Brazil is the classic example of an economic miracle and a social collapse, while many of the communist countries managed to redistribute their way to poor health; high infant mortality; and listless, dispirited populations.

But if either way can work for development, only one of them can work for the planet. Japan has bought its prosperity at terrible cost: though at home an environmentally virtuous nation, abroad it competes with the United States for supremacy as the single worst plunderer of the environment. Fish stocks dwindle in its drift nets; the world's tropical and temperate forests fall to its logging companies; the vast fleets of cars and motorcycles and four-wheelers produced by its industries send up clouds of carbon dioxide around the world. Kerala, by contrast, takes care of 30 million people with very little in the way of outside resources—money orders sent home from workers in the Persian Gulf are its main connection to the petroleum economy.

By economists' standards, Kerala is an inefficient place, full of hand labor that could be better done by oil and by machine, and cottage industry that will be "disciplined" by the open market. But definitions change, and given the environmental crisis to which "efficiency" has helped bring us, Kerala may be more vanguard than backwater. At the moment, America's agriculture system uses about a gallon of oil to feed each of us each day, ten kilocalories of fossil fuel for each kilocalorie of food. It is incredibly efficient in its use of human labor, but very inefficient in its use of oil. Someday, because we either run out of oil or run out of atmosphere in which to comfortably store the byproducts of oil consumption, we may turn to Kerala for advice on a new green revolution.

No cliché is more hackneyed than the middle way, the happy medium—and yet, in environmental terms, it is the clear and only objective. The new middle way will have to define itself in terms unfamiliar both to Marxists and to entrepreneurs. With the environment as its reference point, stability would be its goal. Instead of the linear world of more people and more goods, the objective would be a cyclical world where populations and harvests hover eternally at levels low enough not to damage the soil. Where possessions are simple and built to last. (Not crude—elegant.) Technology will accomplish some of these goals; in Kerala, for instance, there's a push on to replace the old wood cookstoves with much more efficient smokeless models. But technology alone seems unlikely to save the day—even if cars were electric, for instance, there isn't enough rubber and steel to make them for every person on earth, nor enough room to drive them. And you'd still have to generate the electricity.

No, this middle way would rely on inefficiency as much as efficiency. Keralites may need more bicycles; so do Americans, since most of us live in urban and suburban communities that could adapt to pedal-powered transportation. The adaptation would come at a cost in "efficiency"—that is, it takes longer to get to work on a bicycle, but it would spare the planet the ton of CO_2 given off annually by each car. And the bicycle compensates in other ways: it makes you healthier and less stressed, more in touch with the natural world and with your neighbors. Similarly, buses and trains are far more efficient than cars in the way they use resources. Unless they're as well run as Curitiba's, buses may not be as convenient—or quite as efficient in the way they use our individual time—but again they have compensations: the chance for community, the time to read a book.

Imagine a world in which we took our satisfaction from different sources than at present—from small homes built elegantly and cheaply instead of the ostentatious and inefficient castles erected in suburbia, for instance. An architect named Laurie Baker has revolutionized architecture in Kerala in recent years; his homes and buildings were instantly recognizable because to save on glass and bricks he used not windows, but *jalis*—holes in the wall where he left out bricks in patterns, allowing breezes but not burglars to enter and leave. His houses are cheap, and we need cheap housing if we're to house the millions around the world who are homeless. But not *just* cheap. I slept in one of his rooms for a week, pleasant with just a ceiling fan even when the temperature topped a hundred degrees.

In such a world we would look forward to public festivals, not private buying. Franke reports that in Nadur, even though the festival of Puram falls during the cash-strapped spring, everyone in town contributes so that elephants can be rented, fireworks bought, musicians hired. It is a grand occasion; "as the evening wore on, many went inside the temple walls where they sat, prayed, talked, laughed, but did not sleep for the rest of the night. . . . Altogether the formal costs of the festival must be equal to the per capita income of two Nadur households. Puram creates much excitement and joy, however." In such a world, we would make more of our own art, music, community. We would grow some of our own food.

Such a world is not entirely imaginary, of course, even in the most consumerized parts of the West. Very few of us are pure *homo economicus*; we do certain things for the joy of it even though they're economically inefficient. Bake bread, say, or buy good bread from a baker we know, even though the same loaf would cost less at a supermarket. Knit, grow vegetables, play in softball leagues, act in amateur plays, or learn the violin even though we can hear the greatest violinists in the world on compact disc. In fact, most of us probably get our greatest satisfaction from such things. But the way we've set up our lives and the manner in which we worship convenience mean that we simultaneously practice all the environmentally and socially ruinous behavior of the modern, economic world. We ride our bikes for exercise; but when we have any place to go, we drive our cars. We look for bargains on everything except that special loaf of bread, even if it means putting farmers out of business. Kerala is still the opposite—subversively inefficient.

But not, probably, for long. One afternoon in Vellanad, a small village where I stayed, the main street hosted a huge celebration: an elephant costumed in gold strolled the main street, politicians speechified, a brass band with an acrobatic drummer played marches, all to the delight of a crowd that had gathered to celebrate the opening of a new "shopping complex," five small stores along the town's main street. The next day, out with Vishwanathan to visit farmers, we passed a sound truck blaring a message in Malayalam. "Another shopping center will open today," he translated. The average Indian drinks two cans of cola a year, but that may change: when the government altered its rules to allow Coca-Cola to expand to the country last year, a company executive said it was "a major signal that India is open for business . . . a clear message that the Indian market is entering the world economy in the fullest." Someday, like Americans, Indians may drink more soft drinks than water. Already Star TV carries *Santa Barbara, The Bold and the Beautiful, Donahue, Oprah, Microwave Master, Remington Steele, GI Joe, Baywatch,* and *The Fall Guy* every day; and the commercials, both explicit and implicit, are not for khadi cloth or herbal medicines or traditional clay pots, not for soldering together old transistor radios or walking to school.

"The media invasion is the greatest challenge," says Thomas Isaac. "Through it the West is going to hegemonize the world." But he goes on to say, "I am not going to preach to my people here about curbing their desires. I'm not going to go into renunciation." His reasoning, in one sense, is impeccable: it's clearly not up to the poor world to renounce. Remember just how poor this place is: half the people in Nadur village were sleeping on the floor, and 3 percent had cushioned seats. Remember what this world is like: the richest fifth of the world's people in 1989 had fifty-nine times the income of the poorest fifth—up from a mere thirty times in 1960. Fifty-nine times the income! "First World" and "Third World" do not begin to sum up the difference; this is the First World and the Fifty-Ninth World! In material terms we inhabit different planets, solar systems, galaxies. And there is no reason—of morality or environment or economics—that people across Kerala couldn't double or triple their "standard of living." No reason they each shouldn't own a bicycle, for instance, which would mean a change in mobility far more profound than a second car in an American driveway. And no reason they couldn't have more without harming the environment—if we had less.

As mentioned in the introduction to this book, I interviewed Al Gore about six months after he became vice president. I want to repeat what he said: "We are in an unusual predicament as a global civilization. The maximum that is politically feasible, even the maximum that is politically *imaginable* right now, still falls short of the minimum that is scientifically and ecologically necessary." That minimum, it seems to me, is some way of slowing growth to a halt and still spreading the wealth—a painful end to the illusions of the past few hundred years, and especially the last fifty. Perhaps it will not be possible until things really start to pinch.

When that moment does finally come, though, Kerala offers a pair of messages to the First World. One is that sharing works. Redistribution has made Kerala a decent place to live, even without much economic growth. The second, and even more important, lesson is that some of our fears about simpler living are unjustified. It is not a choice between suburban America and dying at thirty-five, between Wal-Mart and hunger, between 500 channels of television and ignorance. Kerala is a fact on the ground, both inspiring and discomfiting. The average American income is seventy times the average Keralite one—there is some latitude for change.

Chapter 4

HOME AGAIN:
A FUTURE GLIMPSED

A few years ago, the Adirondack county in which I live decided it needed a new landfill. The consultants said 375 acres were required, in order to store the ash from the hundred-million-dollar incinerator they'd sold the county on a few years earlier. Three hundred and seventy-five acres of landfill lined with two (2) giant rubber sheets, enormous landfill Trojans to prevent unwanted leakage. Three hundred and seventy-five acres that would need to be kept free of trees, mowed twice a year for eternity so no roots would ever rupture the rubbers. And of course the landfill would need huge sodium vapor lights, left on all night. Anyhow, the consultants conducted a highly scientific search around and about the county to determine the best place for this landfill, and soon they announced their five final sites. And where were they? Not in the southern, urban part of the county—outside the park—where 90 percent of the residents generated 90 percent of the waste. Four of the five were clustered forty miles from the city, at the very edge of the county, right around the mountain where I live. The highly scientific consultants arranged for letters to go out to all the people who lived on the proposed sites, ninety families in all. Letters that arrived Christmas Eve, informing the residents that soon other highly scientific men would be arriving to drill holes in the land to make sure that the waste wouldn't drop directly into a subterranean stream if the condoms broke.

And we were not supposed to fight. Not supposed to fight, because this is a poor backwoods place and they were offering cash. Not supposed to fight, because we're not that kind of people. It's less apathy than a deep feeling of disempowerment. What I mean by disempowerment is illustrated by the following. There was a meeting at the town hall, where the impartial outside consultants were going to explain the mystery of why it was scientific to truck garbage forty miles into the mountains. It was winter, but all the consultants were wearing suits and Italian shoes without any laces. And if you are sitting there in your Sorel boots, you are allowed to get angry for about a minute; but when the man in the loafers talks in his soothing way about the necessity of it all, you are supposed to sit down muttering and figure that it makes no difference—they'll do what they want; they always do. And if you keep talking, they try to make you feel ashamed, call you a NIMBY (which is short for "not in my backyard"), and make you out as some kind of obstructionist.

I was deeply proud of my neighbors: we fought on anyway. This is a backward place—that is, it was only a generation ago that everyone knew how to fend for themselves off the land, and that connection has been slow to fade. People still *live* here, physically and emotionally, instead of residing in that grinning suburban-California nowhere that flows out through cable TV. That connection to the land came to the fore one cold night in February at the final scene of our battle, a meeting of the regional development agency that was considering regulations which might block the landfill. One after another, my neighbors rose to say their piece. Kent Gregson, a musician who'd served as something of a bard to a right-wing property rights campaign a year before, had composed a special song, which he performed for the commissioners:

> They make the garbage in the south
> And ship it to the north
> The county budget pays the bill
> To truck it back and forth

"Who's going to speak for the withered trees? Who's going to answer for the dead fish?" asked Ron Vanselow, who was working seasonally as a forest ranger. Kelly Richards, an eighth-generation native of the area, said, "We get our water from spring-fed wells. We raise our eggs, meat, and vegetables; tap the sugar maples; harvest firewood; and rear our pets and children on the land. They told us we shouldn't worry because they weren't actually taking our homes. But my home doesn't just go to the walls and then stop. That land is my home."

Finally the Reverend Daisy Allen stood up. She is a Pentecostal Holiness minister—she just celebrated fifty years in the same pulpit and personifies "beloved" in our town, after a lifetime of attending the dying, comforting the sick, providing for the hungry. She began her testimony quietly, nervously. "There's a beaver dam there," she said. "It's played a large part in giving beauty and a place for fish. Will the beaver lose their home? Will the fish die? . . . There's no florist where we live, but will we lose or find endangered our trillium; our wild oats; our yellow, blue, and white violets? Will we lose our mayflowers and buttercups, daisies and dandelions, cowslips and adder's-tongues? Will the beauty of the apple blossom and the pear tree be gone forever? Where will we pick our Northern Spies, our maiden-blush, crab apples, yellow transparents, duchesses?" She talked about the darkness for a while. "I can walk the country roads at midnight, able to see by moonlight," she said. "I study the Bible, and I'd like to give you an illustration from it. Naboth had a vineyard close to the palace of Ahab, king of Samaria. Ahab said to Naboth, 'Give me thy vineyard that I may have it for a garden of herbs. It's near my house. I'll give thee a better vineyard, or I'll give you money for it.' Naboth refused, because his father had owned it. But Ahab pretended sickness and his wife came in and said, 'Why don't you eat?' He said, 'I can't, because Naboth won't let me have the land I want.' And wicked Queen Jezebel said, 'Why are you so sad? Isn't it within your power and jurisdiction to take whatever you want, no matter whose it is?' And she wrote letters in Ahab's name. And Naboth was stoned to death. Jezebel heard of his death and said to Ahab, 'Go take possession; Naboth is dead.' And he went to take possession, but God spoke through his prophets and said, 'Where Naboth's blood has been licked by the dogs, so will yours be licked.'" The $150-an-hour guys sitting in the back of the room in their Italian loafers didn't say a word.

And we won. The regional agency rejected the landfill, and all of a sudden the county reworked its figures and decided it maybe needed only ten or twenty acres and could probably rent them from the already-built landfill in the next county. As we were leaving the meeting that night, one of the consultants snapped the locks on his briefcase, looked up at me, and said, "We think it would be more mature if you guys didn't deal with this on such a personal level. We try to keep things on a professional basis." But we'd been right to take it personally. It was the place where we personally lived.

The euphoria faded pretty quickly, of course; a dump is a pretty easy thing to battle, and we haven't done as well when it's a new subdivision under discussion. But the victory made me realize anew the power of aroused people working together, even—or especially—if those people are the "locals" or "rednecks" or "woodchucks," which is the Adirondack term. It felt a little like Kerala. And it helped me see beyond the trees and bears to the other glories of this place. If the Adirondacks were just a walled-off park, the views would still be splendid, and the wildlife might be even better off. But it's the fact that there are people here and throughout the rural East that makes its recovery so special. Long live the beaver; long live Daisy Allen.

And so, my foreign travels done, I came back home to embark on another kind of journey, one that involved invention as much as reporting. Could I imagine some futures that, slowly and haltingly, incorporated the hope I'd found abroad into some truly realistic vision for my home place? And, hence, for places like it around the world? I know that many of the people reading this book live in cities and suburbs, and I have tried to give them much to mull over. Their future is critical; without efficient and lovable cities that have mustered the will once more to be public and integrated places, a hopeful environmental future is hard to conceive.

But because of where I live, some of what I have to say applies more directly to rural areas and to smaller towns and villages. That is, to the kind of place where half the world's people still live. To the kind of place that covers 95 percent of the terrestrial surface. To the kind of place where nearly all food and wood is grown. To the kind of place where the rest of creation must make *its* living.

To the kind of place that, conceivably, some of this century's urban migrants might want to return to someday, were it to change.

To the kind of place where a new politics born from our environmental trouble may yet emerge. The tired battles between corporate capitalism and monolithic socialism have never been about places like the one where I live. At best, rural areas have been granaries to feed the urbanizing, industrializing, modernizing world of both the East and the West. Whether First World or Third World, communist or democratic, the demographic drive toward the cities has been the same, spawned by irresistible economic pressures. We know already that the Soviet model doesn't work, economically or environmentally; the ecological unraveling now underway will expose the flaws in our consumer society's addiction to growth. I sense that anything truly new will come not from the universities or the legislative halls, but from the meeting between human and humus, between community and countryside.

And if such a new politics is to emerge, it will have to come from the people who actually live in such places, people who are currently on the outskirts of political life in every nation on earth.

★   ★   ★

In the past, eastern environmentalism—like most environmentalism around the world—has been a distant and patrician enterprise. City folks have wanted to protect the mountain heights where they spent their summers, the lakes where they had their camps—just as animal lovers in the West have struggled to protect the elephants of Africa or the seals of Siberia. No slur is intended; such efforts are essential. I camped not long ago on a knoll overlooking the old

J. P. Morgan estate, Camp Uncas, in Raquette Lake, New York. It has long since changed hands, but there was a benefit party there that night; and the parking lot was gridlocked with Range Rovers. Out on the lake in a canoe, I could see the light playing warm out the windows of the great house; and when the wind was blowing from the north, the splash of laughter and the ripple of a light hand on a grand piano spilled out across the water, meeting the call of a loon. Parties like that, I realized, had given the loon a place to live— the bonding of the rich and powerful, their sentimental attachment to these mountains so removed from their more ruthless real lives. Nelson Rockefeller, when he was Republican governor of New York, saved the Adirondacks from a twenty thousand-unit vacation home scheme and launched the nation's most far-reaching rural zoning system—thank heaven for plutocrats.

But that sort of feudal noblesse oblige, while it lives on in many conservation groups, cannot guard the future of either the region or the world. The prototype of the emerging environmentalist is instead Jamie Sayen, who lives on a back road in a paper-mill town in northern New Hampshire—a road lined with trailers, where none of the houses have clever names carved on wooden signs out front. He has a big vegetable garden, and a wood stove, and running water—though it runs from a spring in the woods and he has to run down the hill to fetch it. When I first met him, Sayen was on the fringe of the militant environmental group Earth First! He and his buddies attended hearings dressed as animals; one of his friends dumped sawdust on the New Hampshire governor's desk. I remember a cold day at a northern New York pond, which the state environmental department was poisoning with rotenone in order to wipe out the "trash fish" and introduce some angler-friendly trout;

Sayen spent the afternoon in a canoe with a duck-shaped hat on his head, delivering a sermon about the proceedings, which ended only with his arrest on a bogus charge of assaulting a state official. The case was tossed out by the grand jury, and Sayen was spared jail. Which turned out to be a good thing for the northern forest, since he has emerged as perhaps its ablest and most tireless partisan.

In the spring of 1987 he published a map and an essay, "The Appalachian Mountains, Vision and Wilderness." In it he calls for "continuous wild habitat the length of the Appalachian Range which in time could enable the return of unique plants and large animals—panthers, bears, wolves, moose—that have been exterminated throughout all or part of the mountain chain." The Appalachian Trail, stretching from Maine to Georgia, was the obvious thread for this recovering wildness, a "backbone" strong enough to "support the weight of the massive wild areas throughout the reaches" of the East that would be joined by corridors through zones of human inhabitation. Sayen wrote confidently, because he began with a simple assumption that drove the rest of his thinking: the East, and by extension other spots on earth, would be successfully restored when the animals and plants that belonged there could safely return and live out their destinies. "We must consider the natural history of the region and the ecological needs of the wildlife and the landscape, rather than continuing to ask, 'What is politically realistic in the context of industrial America?' . . . We must consider the whole system, not what sort of a compromise we can sneak through Congress."

Following his lead, others have developed similar proposals. As we flew over Maine in that Cessna, for instance, we looked at more than clearcuts. Michael Kellett's small environmental group, RESTORE, has proposed a 3-million-acre Maine Woods National Park, which would be among the largest in the lower forty-eight. All day as we flew, Kellett would announce, "We're crossing the park boundary now" or "We've just flown out of the park." At one point Rudy Engholm, the pilot, took us up to about four thousand feet and turned the plane in a tight circle. "From here you can see about three million acres," he said. "It makes it all a little more real." And it did—it was easy to envision the northern anchor of a renewed wilderness system, a block of green vast enough to nurture packs of wolves and herds of caribou, solitary cougar and lynx, that might in time spread down through the East. "It's not too late," said Kellett. "The loggers have done a lot of damage, but there's still a chance for regeneration."

A southern branch of Sayen's Preserve Appalachian Wilderness movement recently published detailed plans for the Blue Ridge Mountains. In some ways the task in the Southeast is easier than in the North because the public already owns much of the land, through its national forests. Most of the 3.5 million acres of national forest and national park in the mountains stretching from Virginia down to Georgia are still heavily logged and crisscrossed with roads that must be slowly closed if the most sensitive plants and animals are to survive. Big wilderness proposals have surfaced for the Monongahela National Forest in the central Appalachians, for the Green Mountain and White Mountain National Forests in Vermont and New Hampshire—indeed, for all the surprisingly large eastern tracts still devoid of houses, which with changes in management might turn into reservoirs of wildness for the entire region. It is not inconceivable that moose will someday wander all the way down the Appalachians or that cougars will find their way back to most of the states where they once lived.

These big wilderness proposals reflect the emerging wisdom of conservation biologists, whose insight that large is better than small can be traced to E. O. Wilson's studies of island biogeography in the early 1960s. The smaller the island, he found, the fewer the number and range of species. "In the early 1980s people started thinking about habitat surrounded by human modifications as an island," says Steve Trombulak, a professor of biology at Vermont's Middlebury College. "By now, there are more scientists who believe you need large blocks of land to protect species than there are who believe in evolution." As we talked, Trombulak and I wandered a trapline he'd set out on a ridge below Mount Mansfield, Vermont's tallest peak. He opened trap after trap, shaking field mice and red-backed voles out into a small jar, examining them for a minute, and then letting them go.

"There's a real connection between what conservation science is learning and what we're going to be deciding about how to inhabit this place," he says. "There are the problems with fragmentation, for instance—the demonstration that as a landscape becomes fragmented, you reduce in a whole variety of ways the ability of the organisms to persist in the remaining habitat." Frogs may be unable to recolonize ponds where populations have dwindled in the course of natural cycles, for instance, because they're killed crossing roads in the course of their springtime return to vernal pools. "I'm not saying we need to close every road—there are underpasses that can be built on the major roads. Others might be closed seasonally, when animals are migrating across them. Maybe you'd put up a barrier that says, 'Sorry, road closed until July fifteenth unless you live down here, in which case you've got to drive twenty miles an hour.'"

We stop at an elaborate salamander trap Trombulak has dug in the woods. "Here's a wood frog," he says happily. "These can be frozen alive in the leaf litter." He makes a careful note, and then resumes walking and talking. "One of the things that a study of conservation biology tells us is that you don't need all *that* much land set aside for biotic integrity. By and large, species are pretty widely distributed, so you'd only need to set aside about half the landscape for nature. Now, a lot of people hear that and say it's ridiculous, that there's no way we can set aside half for nature. I don't see it that way—that's about what it's like in the Adirondacks. More than half of Maine is for sale by the paper companies. Here in Vermont we've got the Green Mountains."

★   ★   ★

This commitment to big wilderness is dramatic. But the new conservationists are even more radical than that. "Radical" because they are beginning to think seriously about what happens on the other half of the land—the part that people occupy. "Radical" because they have sensed that the East offers a startling opportunity, not simply for nature to blossom again *but for community to renew itself as well.* Under the spell of Kerala and Curitiba, I see everywhere around me the chance for new economies and new politics—for a civilization living closer to the limits set by its place, one that begins to solve not only its local problems but does less damage to the ozone layer, the upper atmosphere, the climate. This vision, I repeat, is wild-eyed, radical, and subversive. A Rockefeller could happily set aside Adirondack wilderness, but to imagine self-sufficient, self-reliant Adirondack communities would threaten everything a Rockefeller stood for. And say they spread beyond the Adirondacks, beyond the East—it's truly alarming.

At the moment, such subversion seems unlikely; rural residents of the East seem more interested in an old politics than a new one. In recent years almost everything environmentalists have proposed has been opposed by a growing band of "property rights" activists. In the Adirondacks when a state committee proposed a series of changes to tighten zoning and restrict development in the park, many of my neighbors reacted with vitriol. Motorcades slowed traffic to a crawl on the highway to Albany, and bumper stickers blossomed on half the pickups in the neighborhood: "The Adirondacker: An Endangered Species." Environmentalists had their barns burned. It does not seem like a very auspicious moment to be imagining widespread social change.

And yet some of my neighbors who blockaded the Northway were battling the dump six months later. The property rights movement is headed by ugly zealots backed by big industry, but most of the Adirondackers who reacted so bitterly to the idea of more controls on their lives were not violent fanatics. Though their anger was fed by misinformation and fanned by real estate developers who had a lot at stake, it came from the sense that they had not been consulted about the new plans for the park, any more than their forebears had been consulted when the state legislature first set up the park a hundred years ago. In those days such feudal power was commonplace; people may have grumbled, but they did not expect anything different. Now, people resent distant powers telling them how to live their lives—which should not necessarily horrify environmentalists, who have, after all, talked for years about local control, about bioregional-ism, about place and scale.

Quiet signs of that emerging political maturity can be found if you look hard enough. At the zenith of the property rights back-lash, a neighbor of mine named Duane Ricketson, an eighth-genera-tion Adirondacker, found himself thinking, "This is going too far. I knew there were people up here who thought the Adirondacks were special and needed special treatment." A few members of the North Creek Rotary Club were having the same discussion; together they decided to form the Residents Committee to Protect the Adiron-dacks. "We went and got a loan to do some newspaper ads," says Ricketson. "It was a three-thousand-dollar loan, and I had to put up my pickup truck as collateral. It wasn't exactly the rich elitists forming a new group." Within six weeks they had six hundred mem-bers: small compared to the antienvironmental groups then domi-nating the news, but it has become the nucleus of a park-wide effort still going strong. "People were so relieved—they felt like they were frustrated because there was so much anger and intimidation if you blasphemed the stereotyped Adirondack position."

Ricketson says he understood, and shared, many of the com-plaints about the old way of doing business: "There was a genuine lack of participation by Adirondack officials. Through the grape-vine, through the media, you get the sense that they're making all these decisions and not asking us." Given more freedom, includ-ing the freedom to make mistakes, a growing political maturity is inevitable, says Ricketson. "We see the second-home development that is going on—but everyone who lives here is willing to admit it's a special, natural place, and sooner or later they start saying to themselves, 'I don't like the way that was done.' It may be twenty years from now, but someone will stand up and start spewing all the rhetoric we've heard about property rights and so on, and they'll be laughed out of the room."

To talk about "political maturity" by itself, however, is insufficient. As in Kerala, the ability to make one's own decisions only truly comes with economic maturity. At the moment, the rural East—like almost every other part of the globe—is whipsawed by economies vastly beyond its control. The look of our landscape and the patterns of our lives are determined by the global economy of timber and paper, and by the regional economies that drive second-home construction. We need something else: an economy that not only doesn't require endless growth to sustain it, but begins doing with less; one that not only stops pitting jobs against the environment, but begins to question what jobs mean and how much money they should pay. An economy that begins to decouple the region from the globe, increasing its self-reliance and sustainability. An economy that puts less crud in the air—an economy that wouldn't change the world's temperature.

Even imagining such an alternative moves this discussion toward fantasy: there are only the smallest, dimmest signs that such a challenge to the economic order is possible. In some ways, that order is hardest to challenge from a backwater like the rural East; we are poor, dependent, powerless.

On the other hand, we have the least to lose.

The globalization and mechanization of the logging industry, for instance, means that it now supports an ever shabbier and less secure way of life. The timber industry still employs a fair number of people, perhaps a hundred thousand in the northern forest of New

York and New England. But from 1984 and 1992 there was a 40 percent decline in logging jobs in the Maine woods, a loss echoed across the region; the big new machines like the feller-bunchers required many fewer workers. A recent Wilderness Society report found that wood-products workers in the southern Appalachians average $15,850 a year—a thousand dollars less than the average annual wage for service jobs. As Mitch Lansky documents in his encyclopedic account of Maine forestry, *Beyond the Beauty Strip*, timber interests dominate state governments, taking large subsidies and paying few taxes. Mill pollution has poisoned the region's rivers with dioxin to the point where women of child-bearing age are advised not to eat the fish. The state even recently issued a warning against eating roe from Maine lobsters, which is tainted with the carcinogen.

What does this add up to? "The North Country is increasingly serving the role of a Third World country, exporting its most valuable raw material for further processing," concludes one study. Mark Lapping, one of America's premier rural planners and a dean at the University of Southern Maine, put it more bluntly:

> Northern New England is now the quintessential end-of-the-millennia on-the-periphery down-in-its-cups Appalachia . . . filled with dying towns, an aging population lacking the "necessary skills" to make it in the new world economic order, and cultural despair.

Such towns, he added, are "chronically poor places which destroy the human spirit as well as the land, animals, plants and water."

Want to understand this poverty? Read any of Carolyn Chute's novels, particularly her masterpiece, *Merry Men*, set in a northern forest town where most of the trees have been hauled off to the chipping mills, where the only work is "five hammers for five weeks" building new vacation homes, and where the poverty is so ingrained that no one expects much more. Those who can, get out; most everyone else subsides into food stamps and bad health and hopelessness. "Modern education is working on everyone to be desk people or people who fail at being desk people," Chute, who grew up in this world and lives there still, told me. "There's no chance for an A-plus in working with old people or growing your own food. There's only desk."

Want to understand it? Read a recent *Wall Street Journal* feature on the rural poor, set in Vermont and peopled with characters who could have wandered straight out of Chute's novel. The reporter interviewed Brian Deyo, who takes home $188.40 a week for his full-time job stenciling logos on hockey sticks. His brother-in-law, Garth Shannon, used to work in a shoe factory that paid nine dollars an hour, but it moved to the Dominican Republic. Now he works in hockey sticks, too, and tries to support a family of five on $5.95 an hour. He's paying for his eyeglasses on installments. The story ends with the two men out hunting for their larder. They don't find the bear they were looking for, and so they debate long and hard about whether to shoot a crow ("edible if you cook it just right," says Deyo). They can't get a clear shot. "Mr. Shannon touches his brother-in-law on the arm. 'It could have been worse,' he says. 'At least we didn't waste any bullets.'"

Want to understand it? Visit Mitch Lansky, the environmental activist. He lives in Wytopitlock, Maine, a town that exists, just, in the center of thousands of acres of trees slowly regenerating from clearcuts—trees that will be valueless for years to come. Those who work in the woods must routinely drive hours to the patches still worth cutting. Even the local cottage industry—making wreaths for Christmas trees—was affected when the timber company that owns the land started charging a fee to anyone wanting to glean balsam tips from its woods.

Those places with decent jobs—the mill towns, mostly—are watching them disappear. Shares of Scott Paper hit a record high on the New York Stock Exchange in the summer of 1994, shortly after its chief executive announced plans to lay off 10,500 workers, or a third of its work force, by the end of 1994. The company also sold off nine hundred thousand acres of Maine forest and several mills. A South African paper concern bought them, saving at least some jobs—but moving control over the land even farther away, to the opposite side of the planet. Such loss of control is an inevitable feature of the emerging global economy, where paper can come as easily from South Africa as from Maine.

That poverty and insecurity gives the big economic players tremendous leverage, of course. By threatening to take away jobs, they sway regulators, cut taxes, elect officials. But that leverage works only so far. Precisely because these places are worked over, because they are among the poorest parts of the country, they are the places where the residents have the least to hold on to. And, hence, they may offer the best chance for something new to emerge. Or something old. Something smaller, more local.

Most of the Americans who would call themselves environmentalists are concentrated in cities and suburbs, which remain, at least temporarily, beneficiaries of the global economy; above a certain income, the desire for real change rarely seems to extend beyond recycling. The emphasis is still on making the system work a little more smoothly, because people still seem to be in charge of that system. That illusion is being shattered in the backwoods East. Most of the people who live here are deeply conservative. But more and more they are coming to realize that their future doesn't lie with the huge global timber companies, whose decisions to close mills or clearcut forests are made only for reasons of overall business strategy or higher return on investment.

As I was eating breakfast with John Harrigan at a restaurant in downtown Colebrook, New Hampshire, he'd glance up every once in a while and make a mental note. As we were leaving, he said, "While we've been sitting here, I've seen five log trucks going north to Canada with logs to be milled. There's a tremendous desire to do something about that—to get all the jobs possible out of every tree that hits the ground. Eighty years ago we had all sorts of factories—barrel staves, axe handles, shingles, clapboards, a host of products from hundreds of small factories. We've lost almost all of that, partly through our own neglect. We have to stop treating wood like a bulk crop, like wheat or soybeans. It's not 'fiber,' dammit."

"Value-added" is the new mantra; instead of selling maple trees to someone who will turn them into tables somewhere else, for example, more environmentalists and community-development activists are talking about making the furniture near the forest. The Wilderness Society recently issued a report calling for a "sustaining forest," not a "working forest," in northern Appalachia. As one example, it cites recent research showing that highway departments are once again interested in timber bridges, since they are not corroded by road salt; the rest of its list includes everything from printing phone books right at the paper mills to building ready-to-assemble furniture. "The labor-intensive manufacture of items such as furniture, musical instruments, wooden toys, and boats can provide economic diversity and bring new meaning into the lives of workers," writes Jamie Sayen. But access to small amounts of capital is a major obstacle. "We need small loans for small dreams," says Adirondack organizer Duane Ricketson.

Tourism is usually touted as the other economic alternative, and for obvious demographic reasons. Seventy million people live within an eight-hour drive of the Green Mountain National Forest, making tourism a commodity of considerably higher value than the logs still stripped off that federal forest. From 1977 and 1989 tourism's contribution to Maine's economy grew at 7.6 percent a year, even as the timber industry was laying people off. In the southern Appalachians, a recent Wilderness Society study found that tourism and recreation in the region's national forests already contribute $379 million annually, compared with $32 million from cutting trees on public land, and that the demand for recreation was likely to double in the next forty years—two-thirds of the American population can drive to Smoky Mountains National Park in less than a day and a half. "I tell the national forest guys, 'If you really want to make money, stop these roads, get the cougar back in here, and make this place the eastern mecca for earth yuppies,'" said Brent Connor as we wandered through the Pisgah National Forest outside Asheville. In the Adirondacks licensed guides have been showing city people where to hunt, fish, and hike for more than a century; for locals who have grown up loving the woods, it's a good way to stay in the mountains—offering both work and the dignity that belongs to all teachers. Clearly a Maine Woods National Park, or a Nantahala National Forest more geared to hikers and campers than to loggers, would be an economic boon to the surrounding inhabitants.

But not all kinds of tourism are so benign. Plenty of my neighbors scrub toilets for minimum wage at the chain motels, too. And too often tourism drives the cycle of development, as people fall in love with their vacation spots and bid up the price of housing or build backcountry homes that get three weeks of use a year. In the very long run, much of what we call tourism depends on people in prosperous areas continuing the very habits of growth and surplus that drive environmental devastation; in the memorable words of Mark Lapping, the rural planner, "the existence of the second home is testimony to the failure of the first."

In the same way, much "value-added manufacturing" depends on people elsewhere continuing to consume too much. It is hard, to use the most obvious example, to make a strong environmental case for Ben & Jerry's ice cream. Though it's provided a certain amount of help to Vermont farmers, and though its social principles are justly celebrated, packing ice cream in small containers, shipping it in refrigerated trucks to every state in the union, and selling it for hefty prices makes the company a slightly eccentric part of the oversized system at the root of our problems. (The butterfat content, however, may be one small way of addressing population concerns.)

Such enterprises are intermediate steps on the long, slow journey toward something else—a community economy that over time assumes more responsibility for its own needs, that begins to look a little more like Kerala. Where the ice cream, if you don't make it yourself, comes from across town. Perhaps the necessary shape of that journey is clearest in the area of agriculture.

It was farming, of course, that first deforested the East; and much of the eastern recovery can be traced to the emerging global economy in food—to the fact that other areas are being depopulated, defoliated, and worked to death by "agribusiness" so that easterners can eat cheap food. Industrial agriculture in Indiana or Chile looks just like industrial forestry in Maine, a herbicided monoculture that values short-term production above all else and is slowly destroying the health of the land. If we continue depending entirely on distant sources of food, we cannot be fairly said to have recovered, but merely to have displaced our impact to some spot with flatter soils and warmer climates. *And we don't need to, at least not entirely.* The intervening 150 years have taught us a great deal about agriculture—about small-scale, organic, and intensive growing, for instance—that would allow many crops to be grown without once again destroying habitat. The East, and especially its cities and suburbs, will never be food self-sufficient; but in the rural areas we can move in that direction.

At the moment, of course, we are still racing the other way. In New York State, for instance, there are only a fifth as many farms as there were in 1900; they cover barely half the acreage. The meaning of such numbers really registered on me only a couple of years ago when I spent a week haunting the animal barns at the New York state fair. Held in Syracuse, it's the oldest in the nation, authorized by the legislature in 1841 to promote "agriculture and household manufactures in the state." For most of its history the fair has always represented uplift, improvement, betterment, ascent. It was the shiniest week in an otherwise muddy year for nineteenth-century farmers, who arrived to see the newest plows, the most advanced threshers, in the center of the state that was America's leading food producer.

These days, though, most of the visitors stream right past the dairy barns and the poultry pavilion on their way to the midway and the stock-car simulation machine and the rock-and-roll concerts and the sideshows. The farmer has traveled from the center of the region's life to a point so far on the periphery that even at the state fair most people can no longer begin to comprehend that life. Visitors clustered around only one animal pen in the whole vast fair, a stall where a purebred Chester White sow lay nursing ten week-old piglets. And even there, when the hog stood up for a moment and rooted around, snorting at her offspring, people immediately started saying things like, "Where's the guy who runs this? They shouldn't be letting that big pig in there with those little ones" and "She must have PMS if she's acting like that."

As I walked through the fair's vast dairy barn, past rows of cows lying in their stalls trying to stay cool in the late August heat, I noticed a chart hanging on the wall behind almost every animal. I stopped in front of one that read

HANOVERHILL INSPIRE ROSIE
5-24-88
309 21488 42 909
342 22040 49 976

and asked a stocky boy raking manure to decipher the numbers. Rosie, said twelve-year-old Bobby Hulbert, was born on May 24, 1988. In 1990 she had milked on 309 days, producing 21,488 pounds of milk or something more than three thousand gallons. The milk had a butterfat content of 42, or 4.2 percent, which meant 909 pounds of butterfat. A year later, milking more days, her average output had dropped a bit, but the fat content of her milk had increased. Because of improved breeding techniques, those numbers had increased enormously over the last few decades; in 1951, when dairy superintendent Samuel Slack began working at the fair, the average New York State cow was lucky to produce nine thousand pounds of milk a year. The resulting flood of milk has put many farmers out of business. Now a new wave of sell-offs seems poised to begin. In 1994 the Monsanto Corporation introduced bovine growth hormone, or BGH, a dose of genetic engineering designed to increase the amount of milk a cow can give by 20 to 30 percent. There's no milk shortage; the only beneficiaries of BGH are Monsanto and the largest dairies, and perhaps consumers who might save a few pennies on a gallon.

The casualties are likely to include a fair number of boys like Bobby Hulbert, who is standing in front of Rosie and continues to talk about his life on the farm. "All the chores keep me out of trouble," he says, very seriously and politely. "What kind of trouble?" I ask. "I don't know and I don't think I want to know," he replies. He and his brother get up at 5:30 A.M. on school days to do chores, but on Saturdays they handle the first milking by themselves at 3:00 A.M., when "it's very quiet, very empty in the barn. It feels strange, different. You have to go get the cows out of the pasture, and it's more comfortable once the cows are in the barn." Bobby, too well-behaved to stop a conversation, was clearly getting nervous: it turned out he wanted to get his chores done so he could check out the butter sculpture and then go to that night's rodeo. "I've seen it on TV, but it didn't interest me," he says. "I like to see things real." If cows increase their output of milk 30 percent—and BGH is now in widespread use throughout the nation—then the state estimates there will be a "need for substantially fewer cows," perhaps only 70 percent of the current herd size by the end of the century, with attendant decreases in the amount of forage and other field crops required to feed them. "By 2000, dairy farms will be considerably bigger and much fewer in number. The rate at which farmers retire or fail financially will be high," concludes the state report. Dairy superintendent Slack crossed his arms and surveyed the shed full of cows from around the Empire State. "The family farm has disappeared. It's just gotten too big for families."

You could argue, of course, that such a continuing failure of agriculture is good for the East—that it will free up yet more land for coyotes and beaver and forest. But that doesn't need to be the choice. Consider an experiment just across the New York border in Massachusetts. The Bay State, despite fine soils in its midsection, imports more than 90 percent of its food; the only crop in which it is self-sufficient is cranberries. But in the northwestern corner of the state, on the shoulder of its highest mountain, in some of its rockiest soil, sits Caretaker Farm.

I arrived there one hot afternoon late in July and found the farmer, Samuel Smith, sitting in the cool of an old barn with his four young apprentices. Barn swallows flitted in and out as the crew held its weekly seminar. "My skin prickled when you mentioned temporal diversity," Smith was saying to one of the college-age apprentices. "It's true—the farm grows so many things, that from May till the fall something is always blossoming. And that keeps a real diversity of insects present, which gives us this protection against disease." The talk continued inside, around the lunch table: fresh beets, warm bread, an enormous salad of cracked wheat and new raspberries. "Most farms are down to one crop, something that they can mechanize for. So they have these huge gaps when nothing is blooming and there's no insects," says Smith. "It's true, sure it is. I just never thought of it in those terms before."

Caretaker Farm grows thirty different vegetables, but that's not all that makes it different. It's one of nearly five hundred community-supported agriculture farms (CSAs) across the nation, a number that has grown from zero in the mid-1980s. Local residents pay a set fee, which at Caretaker ranges from $245 to $315 per family; the money underwrites the farm's $68,000 budget. In return, the members come out twice a week and pick up their share of the harvest. If a crop fails, everyone takes a small hit, instead of a farm family being wiped out. But failures are the exception, not the rule. Smith walked me through row after row: brussels sprouts, cabbage, buckwheat, garlic, winter storage onions, carrots, lettuce, beets, beans, six rows of strawberries, parsnips, kale, broccoli, winter beets, more beans, rutabagas. We stopped in the raspberry patch to eat and talk. "Last year, on three and a half acres, we grew eighty-four thousand pounds of vegetables—forty-two tons of vegetables." That was enough, if people were canning and freezing with some care, to provide ten months' worth of the vegetables for 240 families. "It's not perfect," says Smith. "We still use orange juice, lemons, ginger from the store. We're still tied to the big tit." But it's sure a start, one vision of how communities could take advantage of all that's been learned about organic agriculture and intensive gardening to avoid repeating the mistakes of the early farmers—who exhausted their fields in a few years. And to avoid repeating the mistakes of the present, which involve exhausting the soil and people of the food-growing regions, flying and shipping dinner halfway around the world, and having it taste (big surprise) lifeless and limp.

There are too few such actual examples. But increasingly, especially among the new breed of younger environmentalists, there are visions; the most compelling are the least utopian. Vermont environmentalist Andrew Whitaker recently looked ahead seventy-five years into the future of his logging region, toward the day when the woods are seen not as a reservoir for pulp but as the center of a smaller-scale, more local economy. "The centerpiece of our new economy is the forest," he writes. "Small, vertically integrated logging operations have access to a good supply of large timber, which they take from stump to board. Local artisans are a more visible element of the economy than previously, and are able to make a living from the production of custom-built furniture, musical instruments, and buildings." Farm stands have diversified, expanded, and increased in number—supplying half the food needs of the town; and "New England has returned to the day when it drank more cider than orange juice." The rural marketer who heads to the city "is able to head home with quahogs or cranberries, as his or her trading partner heads south with maple syrup or cider."

No one model will dominate in this new economy—each place will be different, precisely because it is a different place, with different trees and soil and people. But I am convinced this new economy must evolve one way or another, not only to solve the social problems of this poor region but to begin addressing the planet-scale problems we face. Smaller local economies make sense because they're not disrupted at the whim of a corporate board—but also because they all but demand lighter living, less emissions, fewer products. "In a regional or global economy, people can't really take much responsibility for things," says Maine activist Mitch Lansky. "There's no feedback loop because it's so global." But if you could drive in a single afternoon around the forest that will support you and your descendants forever, you would begin to think differently about how to harvest it.

Smaller, more local economies have a history in these very areas. The eminent American historian Gordon Wood, writing in the

New York Review of Books in 1994, reviewed the evidence in a long-running argument about colonial New England. Against the conventional view that entrepreneurial and market-oriented capitalism dominated the region from its earliest days, he cites the work of a new school of "anthropologically minded historians who found that colonial New England towns, far from being centers of speculation and capitalist enterprise, actually resembled traditional peasant villages; they were stable, self-sufficient, patriarchal, disciplined, homogeneous, and profoundly religious." Perhaps "patriarchal" and "homogeneous" are no longer valid goals, but a place where "self-aggrandizement gave way to concern for one's family and neighbors, and community-regulated 'just prices' were often more important than what the market would bear" sounds closer to Kerala, closer to the world we need. "Rather than relying on the market, farmers supplied their needs by producing their own goods for consumption and by swapping or exchanging goods and services within their local communities. They charged each other for these goods and services, but the prices were set by custom, not by the market; and in the absence of much specie or coin the charges were usually not paid in cash but were instead entered in each person's account book," building up an incredibly complicated web of obligations and connections, a system that broke down only when the American Revolution unleashed "all the latent commercial and enterprising power of America's emerging democratic society."

The distance between that colonial subsistence economy and our present situation—and between our present situation and some future community—cannot be overstated. What's more, the domination of the global consumer economy makes moving in the direction of something smaller and more local extremely difficult, if for no other reason than that the global economy sets the prices. I spent a day not long ago at another community-supported agriculture project set up on the same model as Caretaker Farm, and it amply demonstrated both the great potential and the deep problems.

Heartsong Farm lies outside Groveton, New Hampshire, a paper-mill town where layoffs have been a way of life in recent years. A thunderstorm was blowing in from the ridge of mountains to the east when I arrived. In the dark clarity that preceded the rain, the small spread looked as orderly and abundant as an illustration from a children's book. Michael Phillips dashed about closing the sides of the field tunnel where his softball-size tomatoes were already ripe in late July; his wife, Nancy, was gathering flowers from her large garden—armfuls of larkspur and bishop's flower, golden yarrow and baby's breath, which she draped over beams in the house to dry and turn into wreaths. As we sat in the kitchen, speaking loudly over the rumbling thunder, they shelled peas. It was a scene of surpassing rightness. "I think CSAs are a wonderful thing," Michael said. "Since people invest in advance, when you're growing a lettuce you know you have a home for it. It's not like when I was selling to restaurants. After two weeks of baby zucchini they'd want winter squash, and I was, like, 'Winter squash haven't even blossomed yet.' And there's the spiritual aspect, too. Most folks who belong come out for the picking-up-rocks party, or the potato-bug-picking party. Pretty soon they get into the food." Phillips has an organic cider mill as well, where he and a neighbor have recently planted hundreds of new trees. "Saint Edumunds russet, which blooms a little earlier. An apple called the Dudley. The chestnut crab, which adds a wonderful nutty influence in your cider. I have a fruit-exploring friend who goes out in the woods looking for old overgrown orchards."

The longer he talked, though, the sadder Phillips grew. Locked in the North Woods, far away from cities filled with the food-conscious, without even a nearby college town to offer support, he is barely making it. "The climate is difficult, of course, but it's not really the climate. It's the way we set up the system, what we choose to subsidize. The irrigation, the highways—there's no way you can sell a California head of lettuce in New Hampshire without the government subsidies." Under such a system, the price for a tomato is effectively set by industrial agriculture. Just as careful dairy farmers have to find tiny niche markets or else compete with people injecting their herds with BGH, so careful produce farmers find they can't charge much more than the Safeway. "The one thing we've all been taught is, find the lowest price. We can grow food here, but it might cost twenty percent more. If we could get over that pinnacle, it would be good for the earth. It would be good for the community—we could keep the dollars around here. But it seems impossible to get over that hump. When I first came up here, I was coordinating the local peace network. I had friends I was arrested with at the Seabrook nuclear plant. And some of them won't buy my apples if they're five cents more a pound. That's why that twenty percent just seems insurmountable."

Phillips says he may not be able to keep the community farm going. There's more money at the moment in selling dried flowers to the tourists who happen through; the price of dried statice sold to Bostonians is considerably more elastic than the price of beans sold to neighbors. "But even if I have to shut it down, I'm not going to let my ground grow in. I'll rotate my hay, I'll cut it with a scythe. I'm learning to use a team of horses. When the subsistence economy comes, I'll be ready. Then my work will be valued equally with everyone else's."

We are nearer the nub now. Ultimately, along with all the questions about global economies and environmental imperatives, this is also a problem of desire, of what we're going to demand from our lives. That is, you can grow a magnificent farm-garden to share with those around you, eat a lunch of fresh bread and fresh greens and buckwheat mixed with fresh raspberries, and wash it down with a glass of unpasteurized cider still alive with effervescent tang. You can do it in every corner of the nation. But, in the words of Samuel Smith, the Williamstown farmer, "You can't do this kind of growing, this kind of labor, and still have a per capita income of twenty-two thousand dollars like the average American." I know a farmer, who makes $15,000 a year growing perennial flowers for the nursery trade on a tiny farm along the Ausable River in the northern Adirondacks. He started out growing organic vegetables, but the market wasn't there; still, he continues to plan for the day when his small valley is again self-sufficient: he's driven and walked its ridges, looked at its soil, studied its climate. "It wouldn't take much land in this valley to produce food for its inhabitants," he says. "You'd only need to use the land that was suitable." Indeed, the Ausable Valley did once feed itself. "But that slowly died. You couldn't make a modern living at it." A modern living.

What is the opposite of utopian? Let's be extremely realistic, even grim: a community, a region, a nation, a world that paid attention to limits would mute the horn of plenty, plug up the cornucopia. A community that made environmental sense *would not have all the things that we have today.* Its stores would have far fewer items, and far more of them would be locally made. Entertainment would have to be more homegrown, too: spare cash for CDs and books and videos and major league baseball tickets would dwindle. The highest-tech health care would simply prove insupportable over time. Electricity would come from local sources—rivers, wind, the sun—and be used more sparingly. Cars would grow steadily rarer, and buses and bicycles more common. *It would be poorer.*

In certain ways it might be richer, too, of course. Maybe those of us who live in the cold climes would only get bananas, currently America's favorite fruit, on special occasions—but we would have a hundred varieties of apples to choose from, almost year-round. Fewer compact discs, but more music made by friends and family. Fewer tubes and monitors at the hospital—but a third of our medical care costs are consumed in the last year of life, and everyone I know has the sneaking sense that Dr. Kevorkian is, well, right. A solar panel, especially at these latitudes, produces less reliable electricity, so maybe the lights don't automatically go on as the afternoon wanes: maybe there's time to watch dusk gather. Riding a bicycle makes you feel better.

I hesitate to even mention horses—it sounds too much like Colonial Williamsburg, or the Amish in their beards. And yet I have this neighbor who logs with a team of Belgians. He wraps a chain around a birch trunk eighteen inches in diameter, hooks it to the whipple tree behind the horses, and yells, "Get on up there." Hind legs bowed, they spring forward against the weight—perhaps a ton of log—and quickly, in a bound that defines "horsepower," skid it up a narrow path through the woods to a clearing where it can be loaded. My neighbor gives each of the horses, a gray mare and a towering gelding, an apple to chew. He scratches their foreheads and whispers in their ears while they paw the ground, impatient for another pull. This is a museum piece; Currier and Ives come to life. And yet it isn't. It's better than that. My neighbor cut down those birches with a whining Husqvarna chainsaw. He wears an Agway cap, not olde tyme garb. And he doesn't make his living selling tickets to tourists; he makes his living selling logs to the local sawmill. He likes horses, certainly, but he has a wife and daughter to look out for—horses make economic sense for his operation. When he went into business for himself, he could have bought a skidder, the enormous and powerful tractors that roar through eastern forests, pulling logs behind them (and compacting the soil, often leaving a rutted mess). A skidder would have cost him about $80,000. A horse costs him about $1,000. "I don't get a lot of wood out of the forest in a day, but what I get is mine—I'm not sending the money to the bank for my skidder payment."

And it's not just low overhead. Horses don't compact the soil nearly as much as the big skidders or the gargantuan feller-bunchers, which can reduce soil productivity 10 percent or more, and so my neighbor gets many jobs cutting woodlots that owners don't want skidders on. He can't bid jobs at quite the going rate, but he's always busy. It needn't be horses, either. Mitch Lansky, the Maine forest activist, wrote recently about a fifth-generation Maine forester who uses a small caterpillar-tracked machine to clear away his wood. It needs fewer, narrower roads than a big skidder; and its cost—$30,000—means that he does not need to overcut to pay the note on a skidder. "To pay off those big loans you have to work those machines twenty-six hours a day," the logger told Lansky.

I do not want to sound romantic. Careful logging is not romantic—it's hard work. Hoeing rice in a Keralite field is not romantic. Trading garbage for food in a Curitiban slum is not romantic. The romantics are the people still gazing dreamily off into the distance at some ever shinier future—the people convinced that global warming-soil erosion-dying fisheries are some kind of small bump on the highway to global happiness. The romantics are the people writing TV commercials, and I have no desire to write one myself. There's much to be said for simpler economies and tighter communities. But there will be other hallmarks of this new world, too: sweat, summer heat unmeliorated by air-conditioning, tiredness, occasional boredom, smaller horizons, gossip, sometimes stifling conformity. For security we'd be forced to depend more on neighbors and family, and less on pension plans and government. One's mother, one's mother-in-law, might play a continuing role in one's life.

It would chafe; it always has chafed, and after a period of profound individualism, it would chafe all the more. "People have gotten so private," says Elizabeth Smith, who runs Caretaker Farm with her husband, Samuel. "People eat in their cars!" At any given moment, she has three or four apprentices eating at her table, and 240 co-op members wandering in and out to pick up their shares of the produce. "People say, 'How can you stand it?' But I'm a firm believer that we need community for survival. We've just been coming through a short cockeyed blip in history, where kids moved away from their parents with the dream of having everything, where we placed our elderly in nursing homes. We're at the tail end of a time in history that won't happen again, because we need each other. The new models won't be communes—it'll be something more like where you go back to your own bungalow at night, but there are workshops, community centers, day-care centers, farms."

Whatever evolves, it won't be idyllic; no way of life ever has been. Not even the native ways so beloved by the New Agers of the moment. The myth of the noble savage has long haunted this coast, the idea that the Indians somehow lived carefree lives. No one at this latitude lives carefree lives; the Indians had quarrels and wars, and they had long stretches of the winter where food was thin indeed. As William Cronon points out, there may have been millions of passenger pigeons in the air and billions of fish spawning in the streams, but they weren't there all the year round. The Indians, however, did possess one inextinguishable source of wealth: the modesty of their desires. In the words of one early European arrival, "Their days are all nothing but pastime. They are never in a hurry. Quite different from us, who can never do anything without hurry and worry; worry, I say, because our desire tyrannizes over us and banishes peace from our actions." Cronon quotes Timothy Dwight lamenting the fact that Indians had not yet learned the love of property. "Wherever this can be established," Dwight wrote, "Indians may be civilized; wherever it cannot, they will remain Indians." And, of course, in many places it happened quickly—Indians trapped furbearers almost to extinction out of the desire to trade them for European luxury goods, which they wanted not for their usefulness but because "an individual's importance began to be measured by their possession."

I suspect that the tyranny of desire cannot be overcome—that asceticism is, and probably should remain, a minor streak in the character of our species. I don't even think we need to "change" ourselves. All of us have more than one kind of desire already within us; it's just that we've built our economy and society around one particular set of instincts, and ignored the others. But we could find those others again; they are not so deeply buried. One of the most encouraging stories that I came across as I researched this book concerned New York City and its web of farmers' markets, twenty of them, up from zero in 1976. The markets have saved more than two hundred farms in the region (when farmers sell potatoes to a wholesaler, they get about 21 percent of the final price; when they weigh the potatoes out and hand them directly to a consumer, they keep a hundred cents on the dollar). And the markets have meant better food. A. V. Krebs, in a 1992 study of agribusiness, found that New Yorkers were buying twenty-four thousand tons of broccoli a year, most of it hauled twenty-seven hundred miles from California at a transportation cost of about $6 million. In the course of even one day's hauling, it lost a fifth of its vitamin C—a third in two days.

But, as *New York Times* reporter Molly O'Neill documented, the greenmarkets have been just as important to the neighborhoods where the produce is sold: "They are meeting places for children's play groups, dissemination points for public education and community organizations, platforms for local politicians and stages for concertina players and performance artists. . . . They sell fresh food, but they promote community." In downtown Manhattan they specialize in baby eggplants; in Harlem and the Bronx it's cabbage and potatoes on offer; and the markets are sponsored by tenant coalitions and prenatal health advocates. Nationwide there are 1,755 such markets, up from less than a hundred in the mid-1970s. "I hadn't been to Joyce Kilmer Park in a good ten years, it had gotten so bad," Elmira Johnston told a reporter as she bought sweet corn at the Bronx Sunday Market on the Grand Concourse. "Now my daughter and I bring the children every Sunday, shop, make a picnic, talk to folks we haven't seen in years." The green-market in New York is one of the very few places that *feels* like Curitiba.

A few greenmarkets, of course, don't solve the tensions between different kinds of desires—tensions that will be even harder to solve in the urban and suburban East than in the rural areas. Examples like Curitiba give real hope for urban evolution—for a Manhattan mostly free of cars, perhaps, or a Washington whose slums are less brutal and whose suburbs are therefore less popular. But over long, deep time whole cities and suburbs might need to shrink, to adapt at the edges to a more agrarian economy; if we're to grow and log and otherwise husband the land with real care, we'll need more than the current 3 percent of the population on the farm. I don't know how such a transition will work, or what it will look like when it's finished. But I suspect that the genius for innovation that has allowed us to grow so big can help us shrink inventively, too, as long as we've begun to act on some of the other desires within us.

Certainly the transition to a humbler way of life would take a long time, several generations, and at least in this part of the world it would be cushioned by the large amounts of wealth we have built up in the other economy. And whatever this transition evolves toward, it won't resemble Indian life or colonial America or Norman Rockwell small-town utopia—there are technologies ranging from intensive organic gardening to computer networks that will shape something new. I know only one thing for sure, and it comes from the time I've spent in Curitiba and Kerala: a materially "poorer" life will not necessarily be more disease-ridden or ignorant or patriarchal or intolerant or any of the other things we legitimately fear. It could be sweet, too. That's one reason I spent so much time talking about those places: the solid reality of their example bucks up my courage to dream about my own place.

And one reason I spent so much time talking about the moose and the mountain lion in the East is that the recovery they represent seems to me a crucial precursor to any new way of living. Not only do we have our woods back to use more wisely as the economic base of a more sustainable economy, we also have our woods back to help in reshaping our desires. Once upon a time the Indians trapped out the beaver in order to satisfy a new desire for European trinkets, and in turn the pelts satisfied a new European desire for fur. We have, in the centuries since, taken that economy of material desire as far as we can. We've consumed till our consumption threatens the atmosphere and, hence, all creation. We've consumed till it seems highly unlikely more consumption will fill the various holes in our lives. Now we have the chance to back up—to say that we will take our satisfaction not from the pelt of the beaver and what it will buy, but from the slap of beaver tail on the water and from the swamp maples turning red in mid-August around the edge of beaver ponds.

In a hopeful mood, I can take you to places where this transition in desires is underway. Unlikely places—for instance, a converted supermarket in Warrensburg, New York, the town next to mine. The supermarket now serves as the main clinic for the Hudson Headwaters Health Network, providing health care for the people of the southern and central Adirondacks. When the Senate Finance Committee, in the heady early days of Clinton's attempts at health reform, sent its staffers to research rural medicine, this network was the only place they visited. Its founder, John Rugge, came to these mountains in 1974 to finish writing his classic book, *The Complete Wilderness Paddler.* He was passing his days on the riffly stretches of the Hudson near my home when word came that nearby Chestertown had lost all three of its doctors in quick succession. Someone knew that the canoeist had recently graduated from Yale Medical School and asked him to fill in. He said he would, if the town would build a municipal health center. A long history of private medicine was quickly replaced by a quasi-public clinic, and from the day it opened its doors it was crowded—twelve thousand visits in the first year—which meant it was drawing from all the surrounding towns, whose doctors had also vanished.

In rapid succession Rugge opened clinics around the area, linked together in a single network. Most have a doctor one or two days a week, and a physician's assistant the rest of the time. "Our fees are reasonable—they're low by comparison to anything outside—but we don't pretend they're affordable for everyone up here. So we have a sliding fee scale, and anyone who approaches, with any evidence of hardship, gets a discount." Any of the doctors employed by the network could "signficantly increase their income by locating further south," says Rugge. "They're coming despite the compensation. Part of it is just the area. We live in a beautiful part of the country; we've got the river. Our physicians are here because of the natural assets. Everyone here chose this practice for reasons that are extra-monetary." Most of the clinic walls are lined with the landscape photos of one of the doctors, who keeps a camera in his car as he commutes between one rural outpost and the next; his colleagues carry fly rods or canoe paddles. And it's not just the scenery. "Part of the pleasure for physicians is knowing we have achieved a certain egalitarianism. In our waiting room we have everyone—the bank president, the highway worker, the logger, the momma on unemployment with kids in tow. It's deeply satisfying to our sense of what's right." The salaries need to stay "vaguely competitive," he warns; like all of us, the doctors who staff it are enmeshed in the prevailing economy. But it's a small beginning. It would seem perfectly normal in Curitiba or Kerala, which is a measure of its uniqueness. And it has stabilized one aspect of life here, made it less likely that people will feel the need to leave.

We need similar devoted ingenuity in a hundred other institutions to allow us to reinhabit this land successfully and on a more modest scale. In banking, in transportation, in agriculture. Maybe most of all in education, since that is where desires might still be shaped. The town that I live in is 70 percent state forest preserve, "forever wild" under the New York constitution, a great ocean of biology and chemistry and natural philosophy—and yet most graduates of its high school have never ventured into the woods, much less had them turned into a focus of education. No one thinks of equipping these students to someday run rafting trips for the tourists, to work as Adirondack guides in the backcountry, to build boats, or to do any of the other jobs that might allow them to stay here; no one teaches cold-climate gardening; no one tries to make them see the incredible splendor all around them. I took some high-school seniors on a camping trip last fall: though we live in the darkest corner of the East, three of the six had never been shown the Milky Way.

"You've got this incredible lab here," says Adirondack teacher Ted Caldwell, who takes small groups of students from nearby towns out to investigate the life wriggling beneath rocks in mountain rivers. "We take our samples back to school and look at them under a microscope. That's thrilling. Looking at bugs in books is not thrilling." But we prefer the books because they may help kids do better on the SATs. Here, as everywhere in rural America, we educate kids to escape, give them the skills and the desires appropriate to a nation where place counts for little. It's not just that we lack jobs here, it's that we've bought into the idea that life is shinier in the world that comes through cable TV. For every senior executive who wants to move to Vermont and raise llamas, there are a dozen high-school kids who think they're hicks and their town is a bore.

There are exceptions—John Collins, for instance. His grand-father was the caretaker for the great Vanderbilt summer estate in Raquette Lake; he has become the head of the Adirondacks' regional planning agency. But he earns his living teaching fifth grade in Long Lake. The 1994 class contained eight young scholars; the day I visited they were diagramming sentences on the board about the previous week's field trip to Albany, which though only three hours' drive away might as well be in a different world than Hamilton County. (Hamilton County—the last county in the East without an automatic teller machine!) "The buildings were tall," one boy writes. "The buildings were awesome," says another.

"I always take them by the governor's mansion," says Collins, "and then we turn left and walk into a residential area. It's not too attractive to them—the houses side by side, the brick front yards. The kids are somewhat appalled that people live like that." On the other hand, he says, "If I told you the number of times I'd heard high-school girls say, 'I wish we had a mall nearby,' you wouldn't believe it." Solving that dichotomy of desire is the nearly impossible, absolutely critical beginning of the transition to a saner world. We need to learn to take our wealth from the natural glory around us, to recalibrate desire so that we're satisfied by the sugar maple and not the shopping mall. That conversion won't put food on the table, and we need food on the table—and medical care and education. But an awful lot of the rest of what we want is not necessary, and pursuing it means wrecking what we have: the moose and the mall are mutually exclusive. Here at least there is still the chance that the glory of open spaces and the loon call and neighbors knit tight by living on the margins of modernity might be enough to make up for the missing luxuries. As Collins points out, "Our cousins and sisters and brothers who have moved out of the park and live in a high-rise in New York and spend all that money—I don't think they live as well as we do. They have second homes here; I don't have a second home in New York City."

Getting people to realize that *before* they move away to New York City is hard work. "We are asking a lot of people who are informed by the world community through the TV," says Collins. But across the East environmentalists and community activists have begun to plan. In northern New England Jamie Sayen has called for a "Watershed Academy" that would teach "ecological restoration, socially and ecologically responsible business and economics, and provide vocational training in arts and crafts." Arts and crafts sounds kind of dumb, like basket-weaving. And yet it is the arts and crafts of food-growing and tree-cutting and clothes-making that ultimately underwrite every human life. At the moment, they are done far away from most Americans—and done cheaply in every sense of the word. But they could be done close to home, carefully and beautifully.

The same education could also help infect us with a fever for the natural world around us. John Collins's class ends the day by watching, with mounting excitement, a videotape of their predecessors from the previous year's class climbing nearby Chimney Mountain, a climb they're taking the next day. "That's an eagle's nest," says one of the other teachers. "That's eagle excrement." Much giggling, much anticipation. "I do believe these kids have a sense of limits that I think other generations didn't have," says Collins. "I hope they'll take that sense of limits and measure it against the Adirondacks they live in. It's a first-grade lesson—you can't have your cake and eat it, too. You can't have the park and chop it up and sell it, too."

But it's a first-grade lesson the world has never learned. There is no question that "limits" will be the globe's chief topic for decades to come. Every crisis pressing in on us—from the greenhouse effect to population to species extinction—is a question about how large humans will be in relation to the rest of creation. Adirondackers know more about limits than most people: we've been living under evolving strictures for a century; and as a result, we're smaller, compared with nature, than almost any place in the Western world. At the moment, those limits often rub; that smallness sometimes bothers us. But maybe we can learn to find more joy in it, to make it the cornerstone of a decent life—one that could slowly spread toward the suburbs and cities.

The message is already being heard in other parts of the globe. George Davis, a rural planner, drew up the controversial zoning map for the Adirondacks in the late 1960s, after driving, hiking, and snowshoeing most of its 6 million acres. His groundbreaking attempts to let nature and people earn their separate livings in the same place earned him death threats from antienvironmentalists but also earned him a MacArthur fellowship, which he used to launch a vast project in Siberia. ("My enemies always told me to 'Go back to Russia,' so I did," he explains.) Working with the new Russian leadership, he has helped create an Adirondacks-like preserve around glorious Lake Baikal. Inside the preserve, which now extends across the border into Mongolia and covers an area the size of France, perhaps two-thirds of the land is set aside for wilderness. But the map also specifies areas that are to be used for careful logging or mining. "Foreign lumber companies are interested, even though we tell them they can't come in and clearcut," says Davis. "They appreciate the fact that the whole system is laid out, that there's less uncertainty than in the rest of Russia." Others appreciate his work as well: along the Chinese border he's working on a similar plan to preserve the last redoubt of the Siberian tiger; the Haisla Indians have requested a plan for the Kitlope Valley of British Columbia, where the largest tract of virgin temperate forest in the world can be found; in Nicaragua the Miskito Indians have set him to work on the tropical forests along the eastern coast. Against the steady tide of exploitation, there is a growing countercurrent of care and reflection, one that is nurtured by the lessons of these hills.

★ ★ ★

The patron saint of the American West is John Muir. The ecstasy he committed to paper in *My First Summer in the Sierra* introduced a whole new grammar of wildness to the world, and just in time. Inspired by his passion, the first American environmental movement managed to save the last pristine corners of the West: Yosemite and Glacier and the great wildlands of Alaska, Bryce and Zion and the Grand Canyon. And his legacy is more than these magnificent places: his voice echoes on in so many heads and hearts. "Here with bread and water I should be content," he wrote from the granite prominences near Tuolumne in the High Sierra. "Even if not allowed to roam and climb, tethered to a stake or tree in some meadow or grove, even then I should be content forever. Bathed in such beauty, watching the expressions ever varying on the faces of the mountains, watching the stars which here have a glory that the lowlander never dreams of, watching the circling seasons, listening to the songs of the waters and winds and birds, would be endless pleasure." His hymn gathered a mighty choir.

In his day, Muir had an East Coast twin: John Burroughs. They were known as "the two Johns," and in fact, Burroughs was the more famous writer. When Burroughs traveled with Teddy Roosevelt on one trip, witnesses said it was difficult to tell whether the writer or the president was more popular with the crowds that turned out to greet the train. Nearly every American schoolchild read his works in special educational editions; Henry Ford, who kept giving him Model T automobiles, insisted that his writing was superior to that of any author who had ever lived.

Burroughs has pretty well disappeared from the national memory, mostly because the landscape *he* lovingly described ceased to be of so much interest. For Burroughs was the bard of the birdfeeder, the poet of the small and homey. Under Muir's tutelage, and under the endless barrage of photos and calendars and coffee-table books from the West, we have been trained to prize grandeur, awe, spectacle. But Burroughs had little use for the sublime. When he finally did visit Yosemite, he spent his first paragraph extolling the . . . *robin*, "the first I had seen since leaving home. Where the robin is at home, there at home am I." Instead of the vast and unexplored wilderness, he wrote about his native Catskills, where woodlands gave way to pasture and field, where small brooks ran into the placid Hudson. Not geysering Wyoming epiphanies, but gentle glimpses. Not untamed wilderness, but half-domesticated forest, slowly healing from the first rounds of logging and mining. *His* hymn was a harmony in which people played a pleasing part. He recalled watching a farmer "take enough stones and rocks from a three-acre field to build quite a fortress, and land whose slumbers had never been disturbed with the plough was soon knee-high with Hungarian grass. How one likes to see a permanent betterment of the land like that!—piles of renegade stone and rock. It is such things that make the country

richer." Out West, of course, the grazing cow has become the symbol of environmental destruction, as it nibbles vast acreage of federal
land down to desert. And now the feedlot cow, primed with BGH
and gushing cheap milk from her painfully distended udder, has
become a symbol of our global food economy. But Burroughs knew,
and liked, a different cow, one that fit fairly easily into the lush ecology of the East. Many have praised the grizzly and the elk, but few
naturalists—save Burroughs—could have written about cattle:

> Into what artistic groups they naturally fall, what pictures of peace
> and plenty they produce. . . . She is the cause of tranquil if not of
> great thoughts in the lookers-on, and that is enough. Tranquility
> attends her wherever she goes; it beams from her eyes and lingers
> in her footsteps.

If, as Barry Lopez has written, "one of the great dreams of man must
be to find some place between the extremes of nature and civilization where it is possible to live without regret," then John Burroughs
is as important a writer as Muir, and his vision just as essential.
His message has been submerged as we've become an urban and
suburban people who escape to the national parks for relaxation,
but perhaps it is beginning once more to be heard. A hundred and
fifty college kids a year apply for the four all-but-unpaid internships
at Samuel Smith's Caretaker Farm in Massachusetts. There, in
the shadow of Mount Greylock, which was hiked by Thoreau and
which has some vestigial groves of old-growth forest, they learn the
patient work of growing things by hand. "Yesterday we planted the
last lettuce seeding, about two thousand heads," one of the interns
told me. "And then we carefully weeded an old strawberry bed and

mowed it with a brush hog, and then we raked out the compost onto rows." The largest part of the day is spent weeding, says Smith. "If all of us just stopped weeding for a week, and there were a couple of good rains, you'd be overcome with despair. We use our hands mostly, and stirrup hoes." I asked the apprentice, a good child of suburbia, if the world of the farm had come to feel like home. "It feels completely natural to be here by now," she said. "We're all wondering if the other world will feel as natural when we go back."

Michael Pollan, the author of *Second Nature*, is one of the few recent writers to address these issues. His book is partly an account of the greening of his Connecticut home, partly a spanking of environmentalists for focusing too much on wilderness. Pollan argues that "the habit of bluntly opposing nature and culture has gotten us into trouble, and we won't work ourselves free of this trouble until we have developed a more complicated and supple sense of how we fit into nature." He calls the gardener (and by extension, I'm sure, the small and careful farmer) "that most artificial of creatures, a civilized human being: in control of his appetites, solicitous of nature, self-conscious and responsible, mindful of the past and future." In this he is surely correct: it is the middle ground that we have lost sight of completely, that we misunderstand even more than we misunderstand wilderness. It is there, in the places where we must grow food and cut trees, that we work out what it means to be the human animal.

So far, so good; he is a worthy successor of Burroughs. But the wonder of this eastern recovery, and the ultimate hope for the planet, is that we need not stop there. We can have both wilderness and careful garden. We can have our homegrown carrotcake and eat it, too. Even on this crowded coast we have room enough to acknowledge that the human animal is not the only animal.

Pollan writes about stumbling across the remains of an abandoned nineteenth-century settlement, Dudleytown, in the woods near his house. "On both sides of the trail stood stone walls—linear piles, really—marking small rectangular enclosures among the trees. Within each square was a rectangular pit lined with rocks: the foundation of a small house." It shivered his spine; it was "spooky," it signaled "a larger, more insidious threat," the "advancing forest." I know what he means—my home place, too, was once more crowded. Deep in the woods cellar holes mark hard work and dreams. But there's another way to look at it: those lives were wasted only in the sense that the work of any human life is wasted. Now the woods have crept back in and reclaimed those places and, in so doing, have offered shelter to the plants and animals those farms once drove out—and *they* are living *their* lives again.

I have an old friend who lives not far from me; when he was a boy, he says, "you couldn't step outside your house without hearing the 'dingle-dingle' from the cowbells. Even if it was all quiet you'd hear it because you were so used to hearing it." That sound *should* be heard again; there are places in our town where, if the absurd economics of globalism relented, cows would make economic and ecological sense again. But Muir was just as right as Burroughs. It's just as important, here on the edge of the wild, that we once more also hear the howl of the wolf, that ancestral opposite to the lowing of the cow.

Biologists often talk about "indicator species," and in discussing the wolf I will borrow the term. If the unaltered cow and the organic carrot are indicators of human beings living wisely in their place, then the wolf is an indication of human beings learning to accept real limits, to pull back. For the wolf simply can't tolerate many people around; unlike the coyote, which adapts to suburbs with ease, wolf packs need many square miles (*empty* square miles) to roam.

When I described in some detail the recovery of the turkey and the bear and the beaver and the moose and maybe even the mountain lion, the one species I skipped over is the wolf. Save for the reintroduced population of red wolves on one edge of North Carolina, the East is wolf-free. In 1630 Massachusetts enacted the first bounty in the New World—a shilling for every wolf carcass. Eight years later a law declared that "whoever shall [within the town] shoot off a gun on any unnecessary occasion, or at any game except an Indian or a wolf, shall forfeit five shillings for every shot." Wolves were gone from Connecticut by 1837, from New Hampshire by 1887, from the farthest reaches of the Adirondacks by 1897, from Maine by 1904. Once the most widely distributed land mammal on earth, the wolf has been reduced to about 3 percent of its original range in the lower forty-eight.

And yet its return is not impossible. Healthy populations still live in Canada, particularly in Ontario's Algonquin Park and Quebec's Laurentides Park. And perhaps they have begun the slow drift back down. In the far northwestern corner of Piscataquis County in Maine, in the fall of 1993, a hunter shot a large canid. "I was the first one who saw it when the hunter brought it in," says Greenville warden Dan Tourtelotte. "There was no question in my mind that it certainly wasn't a coyote. My first impression when I saw it in the back of the truck was that it was a wolf." Doubters said no, it must be a wolf-hybrid kept as a pet and then released. Parts of the animal were shipped off to the Fish and Wildlife Service's Ashland, Oregon, lab; and after a few months of genetic testing, the results came back. Pure wolf. Quite likely a wanderer from the Quebec herd, only a few hundred miles away. And there may be more. John Harrigan, the New Hampshire newspaper editor, has been publishing sighting rumors for years, and he's convinced. "I talk to the people who run the sled dogs out of Indian Stream in the winter. The coyotes don't bother their dogs at all. But when the big guy howls, their hackles go up."

As surely as the spread of community-supported farms marks a revival of interest in the real work of farming, a new push for wolves is finding increasing support. An environmentalist named Scott Thiele spent last summer wandering the Adirondacks, giving a slide talk on wolf recovery in these mountains to anyone who would listen. He got a death threat or two from the antienvironmental faction ("Why don't you bring back smallpox next?" one man shouted), but most of the thousands of people who came to his lectures seemed open-minded, even excited, at the prospect of wolves returning to the Adirondacks. His arguments are more than emotional; though he shows cute pictures of wolf pups and plays some of their magnificent music, he also points out that in Minnesota, in Michigan, and in Ontario the wolves have done little harm. They kill older and sicker deer, culling the weakest animals from the herd instead of removing the prime specimens as human hunters do.

Yale professor Stephen Kellert, co-editor of the book *The Biophilia Hypothesis*, which argues that there is an ingrained human affinity for nature, has done surveys that show "a real fondness" for the animals, even among some hunters, as "a symbol of nature's wonder and beauty." Harrigan has editorialized extensively in his small-town paper in favor of the return of the wolf and other predators, preferably "on their own four feet" instead of through reintroduction. "Ninety percent of the response I get is positive. A lot of the people saying things about how hunters won't abide wolves and so on are denigrating their neighbors unfairly. I've got a lot of friends who are hunters, and they know who was there first, they know what's part of the mix. I'm talking about a bunch of guys who will run out of camp in the middle of the night in the snow to howl back at the coyotes."

Such appreciation is not universal. In North Carolina the state legislature recently passed a law allowing homeowners to shoot the reintroduced red wolves if they stray on people's land. But most of the fears are irrational—big-toothed grandmothers to the contrary, wolves don't attack people. They like to eat deer and other things that run away, so they don't even go after cows very often. Of the seven thousand Minnesota farms within the wolves' range, less than one percent have ever reported a wolf raid; and those farmers have been compensated, by a state that should easily be able to afford it—since the wolves have drawn to the north country large numbers of new tourists, who go on howling expeditions and buy T-shirts.

In short, wolves make sense. They belong here. If we bring them back, we will have passed an important test as a species.

★   ★   ★

The wolf will not return overnight. Nor will we build a new sense of rural community in a generation, nor will we transform our cities with an election or two, nor will we unwind the global economy in our lifetime. "Let's say seventy-five years," Steve Trombulak, the Middlebury biologist, told me one day as we sat in the shadow of Mount Mansfield, checking traps. "The automobile has been around seventy-five years, and it's taken us about that long to create the mess we're in. It gives us the target of working toward something that needs to be achieved by the time my children die of old age." And it will take longer than seventy-five years for the recovering forests of the East to mature again into old-growth; it may be hundreds of years before once more we find hemlocks growing a hundred feet on every creek bottom, and tulip trees twenty feet across at the base. It will take time, and it will take work; the same people employed now to clearcut forests could, in the early days of this transition, find new work closing roads, controlling erosion, removing exotic species.

What's crucial is to begin moving in the right direction. At the moment, in any broad sense, there is no hope: every trend line, from fossil-fuel consumption to forest health to animal extinction, is moving in the wrong direction. And it is hard to imagine where change might come from. In a *Baywatch* world, who will really want to slow down, to reduce expectations, to undevelop? This is a good question, and with it in mind many conscientious environmentalists have decided to concentrate on the possible: on recycling, say. Understandable as such a strategy is, it cannot ultimately claim to be "realistic." In the real world, the very necessary task of recycling is at best calisthenics for the marathon we must run. Realism, sadly, demands that we recognize the need for deep and fundamental change—for recycling our cars into buses and bicycles.

In the political climate of the moment such change seems unlikely. But we need to remember that events change politics as surely as politics influences events. Which is to say, two hot summers in a row and suddenly the calculus about what is possible may shift. If the scientists are correct about the problems we face, then we will soon be forced to respond in unprecedented fashion to the planet's physical crisis. That response needn't be panicky denial or technological dreaming. There are real examples, some of them in this book, that point out real possibilities. Curitiba is not Oz; Kerala is startlingly real, not a theory or a plan or a dream. Fundamental change needn't take forever. Jaime Lerner showed that quick and basic action can shift psychology and alter behavior: a new dynamic takes on a life of its own. Seventy-five years ago Kerala was a caste-ridden colonial outpost, just beginning its epic transition.

An example is as annoying as it is inspiring, though, for it puts the burden on us to do something about the problem. It makes it impossible simply to wring our hands; despair becomes the refuge of the lazy. There is little question that we in the rich world have the hardest task, at least conceptually. There is so little precedent for shrinking; no blueprint for how you go peacefully and voluntarily from more to less. But do it we must; every signal from the natural world tells us that we now loom too large. And we can do it—the moose wandering through the woods outside my house, the beaver who just slapped his tail loud on the pond, are proof that humans can step back a little way.

Everywhere the transformation will look different, just as spring comes to each spot with subtly different signs and vestiges. In city and suburb, in poor nation and rich nation, in tropic and farmbelt and pole, environmental hope will appear in various disguises. Some places it will come as a sleek new bus or a bike path; in others as a cleaned-up slum, a repaired school, a cry of joy at the birth of a baby girl. Here in the Appalachians, on some not-too-distant day, I will wake up and drink a glass of fresh milk from a neighbor's small dairy; that night I will hear a pack of wolves howling from Buck Hill. And it will raise the hair on my arms, and it will fill me up with hope. Hope that the greenhouse effect might someday abate. Hope that this society might be starting the climb down from over-development. Not hope that everything will be fine—everything isn't going to be fine. But hope that the sky is brightening a little in the East.

Afterword

More than a decade has passed since I finished the reporting that produced *Hope, Human and Wild*, a passage of time that naturally raises two questions: what happened to these places? And what happened to the world they inhabited—did it take any notice of their successes?

On the one hand, these questions can be answered straightforwardly:

Kerala elected a left government, with Thomas T. M. Isaac as a leader, in 1996—this government held power till 2001 and managed a number of interesting, even extraordinary, projects: a third of its budget was devolved to communities, where well-attended local assemblies—*grama sabhas*—decided on all kinds of innovations from rain harvesting technologies to biological mosquito control projects to—well, you name it. Local cooperatives producing dozens of products have begun, financed by small-scale revolving loan funds. The left was voted out of power in 2001, replaced with what the American academic Richard Franke calls "one of its traditional conservative ministries that seem to follow the innovations of the left governments." In May of 2006, however, the left won 98 seats out of 140 total assembly seats, its largest majority ever, and seemed poised for another period of dramatic innovation. There's plenty left to work on—unemployment, for instance, stays stubbornly high. But compared with the rest of south Asia, Kerala remains wildly different: it still has the right number of girl babies, for instance, even as millions of female fetuses continue to be aborted every year across India, China, and much of the rest of the region.

Curitiba saw several of Jaime Lerner's original colleagues elected to follow him in the mayor's office, while he moved on to run the entire state of Parana. Innovations continued—the 24-hour street soon had public internet terminals, for instance. The recycling system worked out most of its kinks to become a model of its kind. The bus system continued to expand. And all this seemed to stand out ever more starkly against the rest of urban Brazil. Though the country's economy expanded steadily under the leadership of center-left president Lula da Silva, the country's *favelas* grew ever more treacherous. I'm writing this in late May 2006—five days ago a criminal gang managed to essentially shut down the state of São Paulo, launching dozens of attacks on its police stations.

And the Adirondacks? There the news is more mixed. On the one hand, the state government, led by Republican governor George Pataki, managed to make deals protecting hundreds of thousands of additional acres of land from development. Some will be added to the "forever wild" forest preserve, and the rest will stay in timber production, but under ecological management. But in the wake of September 11, land prices across the region began to go up dramatically, and by 2005 land values had reached the point where many locals found that they, and especially their children, were increasingly unable to find housing. Almost every town saw many of its homes sold for summer homes—which meant that in the winter they were dark, and that there were fewer people sending kids to school or shopping at the local market.

★　　★　　★

The more interesting question is about what's happened to the world in the same decade.

For the most part, the planet has followed the same globalizing logic and momentum already evident a decade ago. Indeed, we've sped ever faster down that route. The most important innovations of the 1990s were the North American Free Trade Agreement (NAFTA) and its big brother the General Agreement on Tariffs and Trade (GATT) which laid out the architecture for a world-spanning economy. The most important story of this decade has been China's wholehearted decision to join that architecture, with spectacular results. More than half the world's construction cranes are located in China now; the cost of everything from cement to copper pipe has shot up because of the insatiable demand for new construction in Beijing, Shanghai, and a hundred other blossoming cities. The country annually adds 65 gigawatts of electric generation to its power grid—twice that of New England every year. And India is following closely behind, steadily expanding its middle class. (Some of that growth, of course, has come from the outsourcing of a wide variety of American jobs—Kerala's neighbor Bangalore has become a center of a booming information technology economy). Anywhere you look around the planet you can see the same trends—it's fast becoming a Wal-Mart world.

That kind of development has wrought some real achievements—China, in particular, has lifted many millions out of dire poverty. But its limits are becoming clearer with each passing year as well. As more countries attempt to follow the same development strategy (sewing T-shirts for rich countries), they end up in a lowest common denominator competition: Mexican sweatshops close, undercut by the Bangladeshi version, which in turn are undercut by the newest wave of arrivals on the Pearl River Delta. And while economies grow richer, that wealth is spread ever more unevenly, to the point where many people have begun to question the entire model. The Indians, for instance, dismissed the liberalizing BJP in their most recent elections, and across Latin America one left government after another has arisen on the failures of those regimes that followed the Washington recipe for economic success.

More to the point, the environmental limits on endless growth of the American sort become more apparent all the time. Water shortages are beginning to really bite in China and India. The advent of peak oil has spooked many people—with every dollar increase in the price of a barrel of oil, our current system seems a little less obvious, a little more vulnerable. And global warming, in particular, has passed from a future problem to a very present one: the spike in temperature, so far about one degree Fahrenheit globally averaged, has proved even more destabilizing than scientists originally predicted. Everything frozen on our earth is melting; malarial mosquitoes expand their range each year; enormous hurricanes and typhoons spawn on the abnormally warm waters of our oceans. And that one degree threatens to become four or five degrees by century's end unless we figure out dramatically changed ways to live. Earlier this winter the great NASA climatologist James Hansen warned we had a decade to radically transform our use of energy or else "the planet will be a very different place."

Such inequities and such dangers have bred some heartening reactions to the dominant trend—dissent from the globalizing model has spread almost as rapidly as Wal-Marts in recent years. I was in Seattle in 2000, for instance, to witness the demonstrations against the World Trade Organization that turned a thousand disparate voices (sea turtles! human rights!) into a real movement—a movement of people declaring that there were more bottom lines than our leaders imagined. The Kyoto treaty process has united the nations of the over-developed world (excepting, of course, America) in a remarkable effort to begin reining in the use of fossil fuels. And the rise of the Internet has allowed the spread of good ideas far more easily than in the past.

Those counter-trends have prepared fertile soil for a few of the seeds from the places chronicled in this book to take root. Curitiba, for instance, has helped more than fifty cities worldwide adopt at least part of its bus rapid transit system. Bogota, Guayaquil, Monterrey, and now several cities in China have built the same kinds of dedicated bus lanes, and seen some of the same kinds of decrease in car traffic. Lerner travels the world as an evangelist for this and other innovations pioneered in Curitiba, "The city is not the problem," he continues to insist. "The city is the solution."

Some of the radical democracy that marks Kerala can now be found elsewhere too. Porto Alegre, another Brazilian city, adopted a community budgeting process, where local neighborhoods hold mass meetings to decide priorities in their communities, a system that has in turn spread to many other cities across the developing world. Similarly, small-scale, low-input farming is spreading fast, backed by a growing pool of data to suggest that it can be every bit as productive and profitable as agri-business industrial cultivation.

And even in the U.S., the kinds of community economies I envisioned as possibilities for the northern forest have begun to come to pass. Across America, for instance, farmers' markets have doubled in number not once but twice in the last decade—they're the fastest growing part of our food economy. New experiments in everything from local currencies to community radio to value-added timber processing to town-scale windmills pop up constantly.

For me, the example of these places has been a constant goad to keep trying—keep building new experiments, keep searching for new embers on which to blow in the hope that the sparks will spread. The longer I've thought about them, however, the less important the details—the buses, the literacy classes—seem to me. Or rather, the more important the subtle animating spirit of these places seems. The world, right now, is choosing between two ideas. In one, the American-GATT-Wal-Mart model, the individual counts for everything. In the other—the Kerala-Curitiba-Adirondack version—the idea of community is a little more crucial. I remember, over and over, the Curitiban transit chief explaining that in his city "public is more important than private." That's the revolutionary notion that these places thrust at the rest of the world—the revolutionary idea of Jaime Lerner that a city can be made "gregarious," the revolutionary idea of the Keralite left that the key to progress is raising the poor majority, not the rich minority. The revolutionary idea that people in the Adirondacks will make their living in roughly the same place as the rest of creation.

The key question for this century may be which model the developing world pursues. If the answer is an all-out grab for American style individualism, then there's no hope (if the Chinese alone owned autos at the U.S. rate, they'd have 880 million cars). If instead they follow some of the development paths pioneered by Curitiba and Kerala, the math may work a little bit better.

And not just the math. When I think back on my time in these places, what I remember most is the sheer pleasure of life in them. They're not, as I stress in the book, utopias. But we've come to realize in the last decade just how far from a utopia we inhabit. Researchers across a wide variety of social sciences have tackled the problem of whether Americans are happy, and most of their data indicates, oddly, that we're not. Or at least that the ruinous expansion of our prosperity in the last five decades hasn't made us any more satisfied with our lives—if anything, we've grown less happy. The reason, as far as the researchers can tell, is that we feel a deep and abiding loss of community, a sense that we're disconnected from other people. Disconnected, in fact, by that very prosperity, which allowed us to build the suburbs where we live in splendid isolation, and to acquire the series of screens into which we so devotedly peer. By contrast, Kerala feels like a society. The streets of Curitiba bustle—people on foot literally bumping into each other. They are reminders that our notion of human nature—self-absorbed, overwhelmingly acquisitive—is a relatively recent invention, that there are other ways of being human.

In my more optimistic moments, I think you can almost feel the pendulum reaching the end of its swing and starting to come back. Our deep desire for something richer; our increasingly deep understanding that the world simply won't let us go on as before—surely this combination of push and pull will begin to move us in a different direction. Which is why, in the end, it's so important that we have models like these to look at. We need to know a different world is possible.

Bill McKibben has written several hundred pieces for *The New Yorker*. His writings on nature have also appeared in *The New York Review of Books*, *The New York Times*, *Rolling Stone*, and other national publications. He and his wife live in the Adirondack Mountains of New York.

More Books on *The World As Home* from Milkweed Editions

To order books or for more information,
contact Milkweed at (800) 520-6455
or visit our Web site (www.milkweed.org).

Postcards from Ed
Edward Abbey
Edited by David Petersen

Brown Dog of the Yaak: Essays on Art and Activism
Rick Bass

Toward the Livable City
Edited by Emilie Buchwald

Wild Earth: Wild Ideas for a World Out of Balance
Edited by Tom Butler

The Colors of Nature: Culture, Identity, and the Natural World
Edited by Alison H. Deming and Lauret E. Savoy

Grass Roots: The Universe of Home
Paul Gruchow

Arctic Refuge: A Circle of Testimony
Compiled by Hank Lentfer and Carolyn Servid

Ecology of a Cracker Childhood
Janisse Ray

Wild Card Quilt: The Ecology of Home
Janisse Ray

Milkweed Editions

Founded in 1979, Milkweed Editions is the largest independent, nonprofit literary publisher in the United States. Milkweed publishes with the intention of making a humane impact on society, in the belief that good writing can transform the human heart and spirit. Within this mission, Milkweed publishes in five areas: fiction, nonfiction, poetry, children's literature for middle-grade readers, and the World As Home—books about our relationship with the natural world.

Join Us

Milkweed depends on the generosity of foundations and individuals like you, in addition to the sales of its books. In an increasingly consolidated and bottom-line-driven publishing world, your support allows us to select and publish books on the basis of their literary quality and the depth of their message. Please visit our Web site (www.milkweed.org) or contact us at (800) 520-6455 to learn more about our donor program.

Interior design based on original hardcover edition.
Typeset in Adobe Jensen, 11 on 14.5
by Dorie McClelland, Spring Book Design
Printed on acid-free Glatfelter paper
by Friesens Corporation